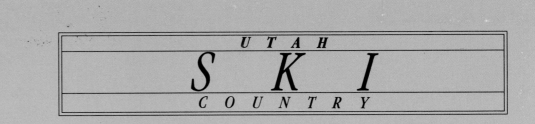

When the hand of the Creator swept across this land we now call Utah, it did so with elegance and grace, and endowed us with a gift of exquisite beauty.

The Utah Geographic Series is a celebration of this vast landscape which stretches for 85,000 square miles across the state of Utah. The Series will portray in words and photographs the unique diversity of Utah's astounding landforms, colorful history, expansive natural areas and vigorous people.

It is our hope that through the Series, Utahns and visitors alike will develop a deeper understanding and appreciation of the wonder that is Utah.

Rick Reese
Publisher

Skiing Alta
Chris Noble

UTAH
S K I
COUNTRY

by BROOKE WILLIAMS

photography by
CHRIS NOBLE
and others

D#232428

UTAH GEOGRAPHIC SERIES, INC.

SALT LAKE CITY, UTAH

1986

Design by Jacoby-Reese Design Associates,
Salt Lake City, Utah
Typesetting by Whipple and Associates,
Salt Lake City, Utah
Printed in Japan by Dai Nippon Printing Co.
Library of Congress Catalog Number 86-050488
ISBN 0-936331-02-X
Published by Utah Geographic Series, Inc.
Box 8325, Salt Lake City, Utah 84108

CONTENTS

*Following page left: Twin Peaks
from the Salt Lake Valley*
Chris Noble

*Following page right:
Thunder Mountain from the
Salt Lake Valley*
Chris Noble

*Near Mount Superior in the
Central Wasatch*
Alexis Kelner

AUTHOR'S PREFACE

The first time I skied was the day after Christmas in 1960. I was eight years old and couldn't wait to try the new Gresvig skis I had received as a gift the day before. I was the definitive novice, never traveling more than ten feet upright. There was something about those short moments between falls that determined my future.

The last time I skied was late last spring. A freak storm dropped two feet of good powder and although it was May, it would have been unlucky not to have taken advantage of this skiing opportunity. An answered prayer shouldn't need timing.

This book is about the time framed by these two days. It is about what has happened to me in the mountains of Utah. When I began this project, my goal was to define the Utah ski experience. I soon learned this would be impossible and to try and do so would leave me feeling inadequate and the reader cheated. This book, then, is simply about what skiing in Utah is to me. May it encourage you to look for more.

Brooke Williams
November 1986

Little Cottonwood Canyon and
the Salt Lake Valley beyond
James Kay

INTRODUCTION

Backcountry powder in Big Cottonwood Canyon
Chris Noble

INTRODUCTION

It is mid-November in Salt Lake City and the second major storm of the season is beginning. I sit in a warm room thinking about skiing—powder skiing. Some resorts are already open and reporting good conditions. Why am I not out in the mountains? My wife thinks it is a game I play, holding out, feigning nonchalance. Perhaps she is right. The anticipation I feel before stepping into the flow of winter's passion may be similar to that which causes nervous behavior in the Arctic Tern in the days before it begins its annual 11,000 mile migration each year. My journey from one season to another is a change of phases; my migration is mental.

Next week it will all begin. I will stand at the top of the first run, questioning my preparation and ability to ski. Breathing deeply, I will push off. A moment later, I will have the answers as the first turns will come as easily—as naturally—as the last beat of my heart.

What is it about powder skiing that has prompted Wall Street attorneys to move to Utah to sell knitted hats so they can ski every day? Why has one Los Angeles real estate magnate devised an intricate plan involving a secret door in his office in California, a car parked at the Salt Lake airport, and a well-stocked condominium at Snowbird? The answer may be found in the feeling experienced in powder skiing, when one can reach across and bridge the gap society has created between the earth and its inhabitants. To ski powder is to be engulfed by nature.

Years ago, I met a man who changed my future. It was at a time when I had heard that there was something special about powder skiing, but I had been unable to see what it was. This man was older, with deep blue eyes, copper skin, and silver in his hair. I had just watched him and his partner make a perfect braid of turns in Alta's Greeley Bowl. I skied over and asked him what it was like. He thought for a minute and looked back, proud of his tracks.

"You know what it's like on a trampoline when you're in the air, finished going up but you haven't started down?"

I nodded.

"Your body is in that state where limbs and ligaments and muscles and all your organs are free from any guiding force?"

I knew the place.

"Then, you start to fall," he went on, "but you're in control because there is a perfect dose of gravity." His flattened hand banked from side to side to illustrate. "Then you land. Your legs recoil and your weight hitting the snow throws up a cloud of snow like a wave of goose down. That's what it's like." Before I could reply, he skied off to find more.

Since that day, I have learned what he was talking about. I have learned that skiing in deep snow is participating in original creation. It is moving through time and space in the grip of wildness. It is the flight of the falcon, the dance of the dolphin. Dolores LaChapelle in her book, *Earth Wisdom*, said, "What seems to be the case . . . in [powder] skiing is that the earth is to be trusted."

I know three things. First, while one turn can be addicting, two linked together can induce visions. Second, there are two kinds of people: those who have skied powder and those who should. And third, whether they know it or not, all skiers long for the freedom of powder skiing.

For most people, life is a search. My search is for perfect snow to make a long chain of perfect turns. In Utah on the right day, this search can begin and end a thousand times. I know something else: a book about skiing Utah should be about skiing powder. This one is.

Autumn in Little Cottonwood Canyon
John Barstow

Skiers
Chris Noble

*Telemarking the trees near Park
City*
Chris Noble

DOLORES LACHAPELLE

"My experiences with powder snow gave me the first glimmerings of the further possibilities of mind.

Because of a snowfall so heavy that I could not see the steep angle of the slope, I learned to ski powder snow quite suddenly, when I discovered that I was not turning the skis, but that the snow was—or rather the snow and gravity together were turning the skis. I then quit trying to control the skis and turned them over to these forces. Now, to begin a run all I need do is point the skis downhill. As they begin moving, I push down with my heels so that the tips can rise just enough for the snow to lift them. As I feel this lift, I respond as I come up by turning the tips ever so slightly out of the fall line to the right. Immediately, I feel the snow turning them and then gravity takes over and finishes the turn. At a certain point in this process, I am totally airborne, but then, as I feel myself being pulled down, I cooperate with gravity and again push down on my heels and feel the snow lift the skis once again. This time I begin to move the skis to the left and once more the snow and gravity finish the turn. Once this rhythmic relationship to snow and gravity is estab-
lished on a steep slope, there is no longer an "I" and snow and the mountain, but a continuous flowing interaction. I know this flowing process has no boundaries. My actions form a continuum with the actions of the snow and gravity. I cannot tell exactly where my actions end and the snow takes over, or where or when gravity takes over.

The more often I skied this kind of snow, the more intrigued I became. In those days there were few powder snow skiers, and we didn't talk about it much; but we learned a lot.

We learned how easily we could destroy the complex interaction by consciously making demands or enforcing our wills."

From Earth Wisdom *by
Dolores LaChapelle*

Dolores LaChapelle is one of the country's leading deep ecologists, practicing in an area of study concerned with the changes necessary to save the world. "Everything I know, I have learned from skiing powder," she says.

Dolores sits across the table from me on a recent visit to Salt Lake City

4

Skier
Chris Noble

Inset: *"Tai Chi is about the
same as skiing powder."*
— Dolores LaChapelle
Steve Meyers

from her home in Silverton, Colorado. Her long, silvering braid lies across her shoulder like a peaceful animal. She struggles to contain her enthusiasm for what interests her—the lessons that can be learned by staying close to the earth.

In 1952 Dolores moved to Alta, Utah, with her husband Ed LaChapelle, a snow physicist who had been hired to study snow in Little Cottonwood Canyon. She had skied powder in Aspen, Colorado, but she soon found that Utah's powder was different, better than anywhere else. There were few powder skiers at Alta then. According to Dolores, "You could tell by the style of the track, which of your friends had made them—a week later. Today, there are so many powder skiers that separate tracks are indecipherable only hours after an area is opened."

Dolores lived at Alta until 1971, when Snowbird opened and avalanche control replaced snow study. She had seen other changes coming. As skiing became more a recreational pastime and less a serious way of life, she had become disenchanted with life in the canyon. But memories of those golden years of skiing at Alta are still with her.

"Menopause," she said, "is a long run beneath a band of cliffs. It drops from the Alta ridge into what is now Snowbird. It is now permanently closed because of slide danger. Four ski patrolmen had asked me to ski it with them the day after the first big storm which ended a three-week thaw. I was the only one who knew the way through the rocks." She sat back and searched her memory for more.

"I forgot to consider the sun crust covered by the new snow. Two of the patrol skied it first and were waiting at the bottom. I was two turns into my run when the slope fractured and slid on the crusted surface. Tons of snow engulfed me and then threw me into the air. The wind caused by the moving snow forced the others up against the trees. Fortunately, I was not buried too deep and they dug me out fast." Her voice tells me that the importance of this moment has not been diminished by time.

Dolores is worried about how difficult it is to find powder anymore, knowing the effect it has had on her life.

"It's unfortunate that when most people speak of powder, it is the new snow covering the packed runs," she said. "While it is better than skiing on ice, it is not the bottomless snow that one skis in rather than on."

The hope is in the backcountry. The pressure on resorts to groom their slopes and the growing popularity of powder skiing lead to the conclusion that the only hope for skiing deep snow lies beyond resort boundaries.

Nowadays Dolores comes to Salt Lake every winter and still skis at Alta when the snow is right. Most of her days are spent in Silverton reading, teaching Tai Chi, and writing. Besides Earth Wisdom, she has written Earth Festivals and is currently working on a book called Sacred Land, Sacred Sex— Rapture of the Deep.

For Dolores, powder skiing is at the core of her life. It has opened a gate for a flood of thought. It has become a source of new knowledge, not only for her, but for the rest of us.

"To ski powder well," she says, "you must turn yourself over to the snow."

SKI COUNTRY

TO LAS VEGAS

MT. HOLLY
BRIAN HEAD
ELK MEADOWS
CEDAR CITY   ST. GEORGE
BEAVER

UTAH LAKE
PROVO

SUNDANCE

SNOWBIRD
ALTA
BRIGHTON
HEBER

DEER VALLEY   SOLITUDE
PARK CITY

KAMAS
PARKWEST

SALT LAKE CITY

SALT LAKE
INTERNATIONAL AIRPORT

COALVILLE
BOUNTIFUL

GREAT SALT LAKE

SNOWBASIN

NORDIC VALLEY
OGDEN

POWDER MOUNTAIN

BRIGHAM CITY

BILL C. BROWN

BEAVER MOUNTAIN

BEAR LAKE
LOGAN

16

Courtesy Ski Utah

I. SKIING THE RESORTS

CENTRAL WASATCH
NORTHERN WASATCH
SOUTHERN UTAH

Salt Lake International Airport
Frank Jensen

Sunset over the Salt Lake Valley
James Kay

Chances are that anyone coming to Utah to ski for the first time will have been emotionally worked over by the promotional literature that leaves the state by the trainload. The people who create those brochures are professionals, and they know what makes people react—in this case, photographs of skiers in powder snow; of the lone figure in an immense bowl, his tracks the only sign of human life; or of a model in a wave of snow, with only her hands and smiling face visible above the white outburst.

The pictures are real: nothing has been done to touch them up. The freedom of powder skiing is accurately portrayed. What is not accurate is the idea we are left with: that from the top of any lift, gondola, or tramway, skiers can look down on an endless, trackless bowl covered with tons of deep, cloudlike, in-your-face snow. But the first run will convince even the most optimistic that making first tracks in a bowl within the boundaries of a ski area is a dream. If the stars line up and you find yourself in the

right place on the right day, the dream may transform into the experience of a lifetime. But don't bet on it. What you see in the brochures are the highlights. What you don't see are all the days the photographer spent waiting for the sun, the snow, and the right person to do the right thing. In a sense, ski photographers are making it tough on themselves. The more they sell powder pictures, the more skiers are seduced into looking for powder, which makes it tougher to find. But snow is renewable and they're still making it, especially in Utah's Wasatch Range.

The Wasatch Mountains hang over the Salt Lake Valley like a huge wave, nearly curling, ready to break. The range extends from Salt Creek Canyon, east of Nephi in central Utah, to the Idaho state line. The steepness of the west edge of the range is due largely to the displacement of the Wasatch Fault, which runs north and south across this part of the state. The impressive peaks are the result of the glaciation that occurred during the Pleistocene Era, the geologic period that

began about one million years ago. These mountains rise some 7,000 feet from the floor of the Salt Lake Valley.

Fast-moving Pacific fronts gain momentum across the Great Basin, absorb prodigious amounts of moisture from the Great Salt Lake, and slam into the abrupt western wall of the range, emptying the cooled lake water onto the mountains in the form of snow.

Think about it: a glacier 1,000 feet thick moving slowly down a steep canyon, depositing huge blocks of ice into an enormous body of water where they float away in the form of icebergs. Frank DeCourtin of the Utah Museum of Natural History says that this process may have been occurring in the Central Wasatch as late as 30,000 years ago.

A phenomenon known as the "lake effect" is responsible for the snow conditions found in the Central Wasatch. This orographic lifting is the process whereby winds laden with moisture from the lake are forced to rise to clear the mountains. Clouds form and snow falls. This same force has been at work since the mountains were formed. The Great Salt Lake as we know it is one-twentieth the size of Lake Bonneville which filled the Salt Lake Valley 10,000 years ago and fueled the mighty glacial periods. The storms affecting the mountains today are insignificant in comparison.

The canyons that make up Ski Country in the Central Wasatch are Parley's to the

east and Big Cottonwood and Little Cottonwood to the south. These canyons are so close to each other that they all can be skied in the same day. There is a company, the Interconnect Adventure, that takes skiers to as many as five resorts in the three canyons in six hours.

How can three canyons that are located so close to each other be so different? Little Cottonwood Canyon is U-shaped. It was carved by a glacier spawned from the giant snowfield that formed at the top of the canyon in the Albion Basin. Added snow and cold from the lake effect caused the glacier to expand and move down the canyon, its ice and rocks grinding away at the granite walls. At its largest, this glacier stretched the full length of the canyon, terminating at Lake Bonneville.

To the north is Big Cottonwood Canyon, which stream erosion has formed in the shape of a V. Halfway up the canyon, near an area known as the Spruces, the canyon is U-shaped, indicating that a glacier moved only

this far toward the valley before melting. This glacier was born in the Brighton Bowl which is much smaller than the one spawning the Little Cottonwood glacier. This limited space held less snow, stunting the growth of the Big Cottonwood glacier. The glacier did move down the canyon, but the climate warmed before it had moved far.

On the wide, gentle, eastern side of the Wasatch Range where the Park City ski resorts are located, the effect of the lake is less significant. The storms have already dropped much of their moisture on the west faces by the time they reach the Park City area. As a result, the mountains around Park City have an average snowfall of 350 inches while Alta averages 500 inches.

Skiing in the Central Wasatch depends more on the lake effect than on the elevation of the mountains. Although the higher summits of the Mount Nebo complex to the south and the Uinta Range to the east attract some skiers, they get less snow and contain no resorts.

Twin Peaks Wilderness
James Kay

Utah's Central Wasatch looms above Salt Lake City
Alexis Kelner

ALTA

Alta's Albion Lift and Mount Superior
Patrick McDowell

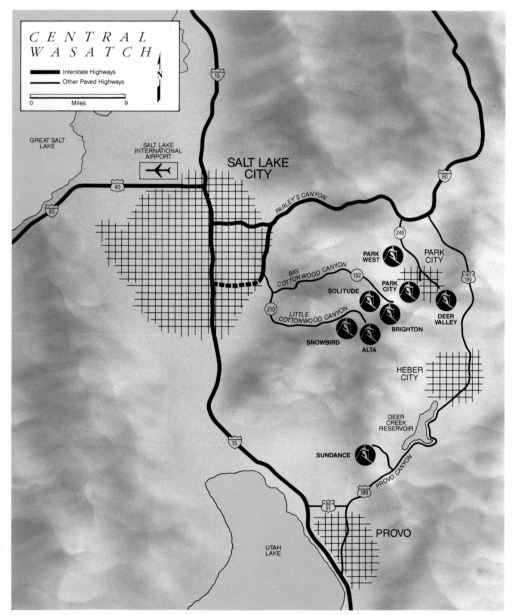

The first ski lift in the Wasatch Range—and the second in the United States—was installed at Alta in 1938. Alta was already known for its snow, but only because of the difficulties it caused the miners who worked in the Emma, Flagstaff, North Star, and any of 3,500 other claims that had been staked since 1864 when silver was discovered. Many avalanches had roared down the steep gullies causing death and destruction to anything in their paths. Dreams of fortunes diluted threats of danger, and people flocked to Alta in typical boom town fashion. By 1872 the population was 5,000. According to Ruth Winder Robertson in her book, *This Is Alta,* the town consisted of one hundred eighty buildings, housed seven restaurants, two boarding houses, three general merchandizing stores, a school, a blacksmith shop, two assayers, four doctors, a minister, a lawyer, three breweries, and twenty-six saloons. The heyday of mining lasted until the turn of the century when the surface finds were exhausted and further tunneling into the mountain produced more water than ore. For twenty-five years, Alta sputtered between small booms until it was finally laid to rest by the Great Depression. By that time George Watson had accumulated a vast landholding in the form of mining claims, and he hung onto the dream that Alta would be reborn. In 1936 the canyon came to life, though not in the form Watson had expected. In *The Avalanche Hunters* Montgomery Atwood tells what happened: *Alf Engen and Felix Kozial had the vision and courage to recommend the development of Alta for winter recreation*

Alta, Utah
Chris Noble

Alta, Utah
Chris Noble

The Skiing. Alta does have some machine-packed beginner and intermediate slopes, but the area is best known for its powder and alpine skiing. At Alta, alpine refers to areas above timberline where the slopes are steep and open, and the snowfall is heavy. In fresh snow, skiing on Sunspot, Greeley Bowl, High Rustler, and Wildcat is as good as you can find. Alta may have the best and most consistent snow in the world; it piles as deep as fifteen feet in the spring.

The Facility. Eight double chair lifts provide access to this mountain with its base at 8,500 feet and a high point of 10,550 feet. There are two mid-mountain restaurants and a ski school that teaches the American Technique and special deep powder lessons.

Location. Thirty-three miles southeast of Salt Lake City International Airport, up Little Cottonwoood Canyon on State Highway 210.

Annual Snowfall. 500 inches.

Season. Mid-November to May.

ALF ENGEN

Alf Engen
Courtesy Alta Ski Area

If there is a spirit of skiing, Alf Engen embodies it. In the fifty years Alf has been skiing in Utah he has reached the stature of the mountains themselves—permanent, expressive, and a vital element without which skiing here could not exist.

In 1935 Alf was working for the Civilian Conservation Corps in Big Cottonwood Canyon. He was given the assignment to ski over Catherine Pass to Alta to check out future projects. Skiing down through the massive bowls in deep and light snow, Alf forgot his intentions. He was overcome by the idea that Alta had the potential to be one of the world's best ski areas.

At that same time, interest in the tourist aspect of skiing was growing in the Chamber of Commerce. Sun Valley was considering their first lift, and the potential for outside money spent on skiing in Utah seemed great.

George Watson had similiar ideas. At the time, Watson was not only mayor of Alta, but he also owned most of the land in mining claims. He made the decision necessary to shift Alta's emphasis from mining to skiing when he deeded his landholdings to the Forest Service.

While we talked, Alf seemed like Santa, less beard and belly. He laughed and smiled, leaned back and stretched his shoulders while he remembered. But when the conversation turned to Mayor George Watson, Alf got serious. "George Watson is the hero of Utah skiing," he told me. "Without the land, this (he held out his arms as if to surround the entire development) would have never been possible."

Alf and Felix Kozial, a Forest Service field supervisor with considerable vision, made many trips to Alta during the next few years. In 1938, after a great deal of skiing and planning and hard work, Alta opened its first lift.

In the half century since, Alta has been the source of many stories. I prodded Alf for memories of endless runs in waist deep powder under bunting blue skies. "There have been many of those," he told me. "We used to have storms that would drop fifty inches of snow. It would take days to open the roads. We would be stuck up here with nothing to do but ski." The twinkle in his eye turned to a spark. "I can remember skiing down High Rustler making only a few turns because the snow was so deep. We would have to stop often to come up for air." The memories Alf volunteered were about teaching and people.

"I've had two careers—competition and teaching," he told me. "The teaching has been my best and the most rewarding. I love people and I'm in the business of dealing with people who have a choice about what they do." Alf spoke about teaching people from business and government. "I've learned a great deal about the world from them," he said. I thought about how much of the world they have learned from Alf and wondered about the potential of holding summit meetings at Alta, inbetween ski sessions.

Alf Engen still skis and teaches every day. I asked him about retirement. "What would I retire to?" he said. "This is the greatest life in the world."

And Alta—Alf knows it will grow some, but feels the Forest Service will not let things get beyond their control. When Alf talks about Alta, it's like listening to long-married people talk about each other. Everything is known but the surprises and excitement happen during moments of changing moods. "There is not a place on earth as beautiful," he says. "I love Alta deeply, because of her beauty and her variation of terrain."

There are reasons why people ski. And there are unexpected results. While some may see the sport as full of hype and pomp and littered by egos, there is more to it, much more. At 8:15 every morning in his office off the ski school meeting room you can find, wrapped in red turtleneck and blue bibs, the core of what is right about skiing. Alf Engen is the ageless illustration of what is possible when mountains and snow and people meet. Perhaps, he is one of our greatest natural resources.

regardless of its grisly history. On the spot they made a unique decision that has guided the advance of western skiing into the alpine zone ever since.

In 1937, declaring that "Alta will be reborn on skis," George Watson deeded 1800 acres of his land over to the Forest Service.

Alta is the scene of my first memories of powder skiing. When I was eight years old, my father took me and my six-year-old brother to Alta every weekend. He would leave us at the bottom of the Rustler Lodge rope tow which we would ride up at least fifty times so we could ski down the hundred-foot-long hill. At about noon, he would show up, sporting a grin and covered head-to-foot with snow. I remember his mumbling between chuckles about how he would have been back sooner but it took him so long to find the ski he lost in the bottomless snow. Sure. I never believed him then, but I do now.

Nowadays skiing powder at Alta is a game of chutes and ladders. The chutes are everywhere, but unless you happen to be one of the first on the lift after two feet of new snow have fallen, you're going to have to climb for it. Making your own ladders off in any direction from the top of any lift is simply a matter of knowing where you want to go and climbing to get there. Sometimes, knowing where to go is the most difficult part. My advice is to follow the locals. They are easy to find. They may be seen standing in line laughing and joking even during the most severe storms. Usually they wear a season pass tucked in their goggle band. They might be

using an unmatched pair of poles. It is the locals who are seen breaking the trail on high traverse to some unknown place. Don't just stand there scanning your trail map for a clue; follow them.

To many, locals seem to live a charmed life. In reality, most of them work hard at less-than-glamorous jobs so they can be where they are. In all of their pasts, they have done some serious shuffling of priorities. They have determined that skiing powder is high on their list, up there near personal freedom and fitness. Locals are serious skiers.

Eileen Olson and Murray Schart are locals. They can be seen skiing at Alta on almost any day. Formerly a professional figure skater, Eileen gave up fame and fortune when she moved to Alta five years ago to become a waitress and to ski. Now she migrates between Alta and California where she spends the summers working and racing bicycles. Her mind is ablur with new ideas about people getting along with each other and their environment. Even the immensity of Alta cannot contain her spirit. Murray works for the railroad building track, which is his idea of good work. When the winter layoffs come, his co-workers go home to darkened rooms and worried families, hoping for relief. Murray goes to Alta. These two locals have made a commitment to the future by celebrating the present and honoring and building on the past. The attitude with which they live their lives is as refreshing as peppermint breath.

The day the three of us skied together, we got a late start—too late, I thought—to find

any untracked powder. Stonecrusher, Eagles Nest, Greeley Bowl, and many other standard routes had already been cut up by fanatics who hurried up the canyon to be on the first chair. Midway through the first run, I was pleasantly surprised. Murray and Eileen showed me the variations they knew. It was apparent that many of the days these people had skied Alta were spent in exploration. We spent the day skirting the rocks and trees which formed diversion walls around secret powder stashes. Murray and Eileen knew where the best powder would be. And they knew what was skied yesterday and the day before that.

At one point, I found myself sneaking through tight places in the trees, trying to keep up and not get lost. We had passed several runs that looked great to me, but Eileen and Murray knew something I didn't. I caught up with them standing at the top of a huge opening, wide and dropping like a rock all the way to the bottom. There were two other tracks—other locals.

While informal, the orientation provided by the locals is something special at Alta. It comes complete with suggestions about technique, equipment, and with wonderful stories. While this service is free, there is a catch. Afterwards, you may be slightly depressed for a while, wondering about the decisions you've made and whether where you are is where you had hoped you would be. Don't worry, it will probably pass, but "local color" will have taken on a whole new meaning.

If there is something unsettling about skiing in Utah, it is the threat of avalanches. Utah Department of Transportation officials and ski area operators are well aware of this and have hired the most highly qualified experts in the field of snow safety to deal with this persistent problem.

"Little Cottonwood Canyon is closed until approximately 9:30." This statement is heard on radio stations a few times each winter on mornings after a significant snowstorm. Unfortunately, there are those who don't hear it and race to be the first in line at the ticket window, but find themselves, instead, stopped at the red gate at the canyon's bottom. Patience is a rare commodity in these lines: skiers know there is new snow and are chomping to get at it. Some are certain that the reason for the delay is that the guy who drives the plow got up late. Here's what really happened.

Three or four times during the night before such a closing, Bill Hamilton or Onno Weiringa, snow safety specialists at Alta, get up to watch it snow. They know from experience what the intensity of the storm means in terms of the action required. They may check to see how the new snow is bonding to the old, and they take mental notes about the strength of the wind. At 4:00 a.m., they meet to discuss which of their many pre-planned courses of action is appropriate. They check with the weather station on the mountain. In this instance, the storm's physical characteristics, plus large doses of intuition and experience, tell them it is going to be one of those days. First, they call the Forest Service and the Department of Transportation to tell them the road must be shot. This means that from a point on Peruvian Ridge, trained personnel will fire rounds from a 75 mm recoilless rifle into predetermined places on the slide paths that threaten the road. This is to convince the mountain to adhere to the Chamber of Commerce policy of no avalanches after 9:00 a.m., when the canyon opens for business. Onno and Bill and the snow safety people with the Department of Transportation have the responsibility to see that any slides coming off the north side of Little Cottonwood Canyon do so during this time period. The recoilless rifle provides encouragement.

Phone calls are made to ski patrol members who will check for stability on the ski runs. At 5:30 the first team follows a safe route to the area where explosive hand charges are stashed. At 6:30 the teams pick up their explosives and begin to move along their routes. They can hear the quick thunder of the recoilless rifle in the distance. In all the known slide paths within the resort, the teams do ski checks, belaying one another to see if the snow stays where it fell. Where conditions make it too dangerous to ski in certain areas, dropped hand charges expose any instability. The theory is that if an area can be skied by two or three people or sustain a small explosion without sliding, it is probably safe. ("Probably" is what makes this business so interesting.) For the areas above the resort, the team uses an avalauncher, a piece of equipment designed to hurl small charges into areas too dangerous or too remote for the ski patrol to get to.

While this activity is taking place on the ski slopes, the induced avalanches cover the road with snow and have to be cleared before traffic can be allowed in the canyon. As the snow plows start down the canyon, the ski patrol puts "Area Closed" signs on ski slopes where avalanches remain likely.

There is one more step. As the plows finish and the gate is opened, cars carrying the final insurance against avalanches race up the canyon. "Our goal," says Onno, "is to get as much of the mountain skied as possible. Skier compaction is the best form of avalanche control."

Onno and Bill have been doing this job at Alta for fourteen winters. During that time, they have not learned how to eliminate avalanches, only how to live with them. The system works. Their record is remarkable.

Opposite above left: Ski patrol aiming Avalauncher at Park City's Jupiter Peak
Chris Noble

Opposite above center: Avalanche gun
John Barstow

Opposite above right: Avalanche debris
Patrick McDowell

Opposite below: Shooting avalanches
John Barstow

Left above: Snowbird tram and American Fork Twin Peaks
Alexis Kelner

Right above: Skiing Snowbird
James Kay

Left below: Snowbird tram
Chris Noble

Right below: Snowbird
Frank Jensen

At the top of the Wildcat Lift at Alta there is a rope with a sign on it designating an area boundary. During the late 1950s, Ted Johnson would ski under that rope and return to the lodge with incredible stories about the fairyland that existed just beyond what was familiar to most powder skiers.

Ted saved the money he earned managing the Alta Lodge until 1965 when he had stockpiled enough to buy the Blackjack Mining Claim at the base of Peruvian Gulch. His original idea was to build a lodge on the claim to extend the operations of Alta. But bigger plans exploded in his mind when he was given the option to buy the Snowbird Mining Claim adjacent to Blackjack. By this time he knew that the Peruvian Gulch and Gad Valley were more than enough to provide skiing for a complete resort, independent of Alta.

Johnson spent years organizing and looking for financial partners. In October 1969 he was at a cocktail party in Vail and happened to meet Dick Bass, Texas oilman, rancher, and member of Vail's board of directors. It was the perfect combination. When they opened Snowbird in 1971, Utah entered the modern age of tourist-supported, destination skiing.

"Be patient," you tell your closest friends who ask for your secrets for finding powder now at Snowbird. They expect you to name names and little-known routes, but you can't. There aren't many secrets about powder anymore.

Patience pays off on that day you've been waiting for. The night before a storm dropped sixteen inches. The morning is cloudless. The first runs you take are anticipatory, without circumstance. Only the main runs are open. You ski them fast, stealing five turns whenever possible in the ungroomed spaces. Your body is skiing, but your mind is eager for the ski patrol to open the areas where the untracked snow is waiting on steep slopes.

It's 11:00 a.m. You ride the tram to the top of Hidden Peak, where you and a hundred others exit to the sound of two hundred stamping boots. In a minute most have stepped into their skis, adjusted their goggles, and headed off in search of powder. You hesitate, with one eye on the view and the other on the door of the patrol hut. If your hunch and experience have mixed properly, you will soon see a patrolman emerge, ready to open the runs indicated on the ski map with golden triangles. To many, the triangles symbolize caution, but to you they mean powder, steep and deep.

The patrolman comes out, his eyes adjust to the intensity of the sun as he checks to see that most of the skiers have headed for the bottom. It is at that time, between the arrival of the two trams, that it is best to open the remaining runs. If something is amiss and there is a slide, there won't be many people involved. You follow the patrolman down the Cirque Traverse, hoping that your patience has paid off and he will flip the sign that has kept you and others from skiing Great Scott, Silver Fox, or the upper Cirque. You used to be angry about the control the ski patrol had over your skiing, but time and experience have taught you to trust the judgment of these people.

You watch as the patrolman stops, looks around, and waits as if for some inner voice to either give him the grand go-ahead or caution him against what he is about to do. Finally he flips the sign and you lunge as if he had signalled for a race to begin. Carefully, you pick a route you know well between the trees and rock outcroppings until you are standing at the top of Great Scott. Your tracks will be first. You hesitate, taking deep breaths. This run must be perfect. You know that if you come here on your next run, this snow will have been cut to shreds by those who will come after you.

Pushing off, you know, once again, the feeling that comes when expectation meets reality. When you reach the bottom, you look back. For a second, your tracks are perfect, but then they are broken by six other skiers. The search continues.

SNOWBIRD INFORMATION

The Skiing. Snowbird consists of two north-facing bowls with 1,900 skiable acres, fifty percent rated as advanced/expert, thirty percent rated as intermediate, and twenty percent rated as beginner/novice. This area has a good mix of open-bowl, steep-chute, tree, and machine-packed skiing on an always dependable base.

The Facility. Seven double chair lifts and a Garaventa jigback aerial tramway transport 8,810 skiers an hour. Elevation ranges from 7,900 feet at the base to 11,000 feet at the top of Hidden Peak. Snowbird Village houses dozens of restaurants and shops, and four lodges offer state-of-the-art accommodations. The Snowbird Ski School is one of the finest in the United States, offering lessons for everyone from children and first-time skiers to experts learning the finer points of skiing powder. Ski school director Junior Bounous is known in powder skiing circles as one of the best in the world. Mountain Experience, the local guide service, offers visitors the opportunity to ski Utah powder under the tutelage of experts.

Location. Thirty-one miles southeast of the Salt Lake International Airport and twenty-six miles from the center of the city, six miles up Little Cottonwood Canyon.

Annual Snowfall. 500 inches.

Season. November 23 to June 15.

SNOWBIRD EXPANSION

For the past fifteen years, the owner of Snowbird has been drooling over the possibility of expanding the resort into White Pine Canyon to the west. In 1982 Snowbird submitted a conceptual plan to the Forest Service showing three lifts serving the White Pine area. In 1985 the Forest Service completed a master plan for the Wasatch Range that deferred a decision on White Pine until additional studies could be completed. These studies will take the form of an Environmental Impact Assessment (EIA) that will determine the effect that such a development would have on the natural features of the area as well as on the hiking and backcountry skiing that is currently taking place in the White Pine drainage. The EIA will also determine whether the Little Cottonwood road could handle the traffic which would accompany additional development. If the Forest Service believes that this development would have a significant effect on the canyon, an Environmental Impact Statement will be required.

At first glance, development into White Pine would add to the stash of lift-served powder. A closer look might show something else. My own Powder Impact Study shows that people are skiing powder in White Pine all the time. Backcountry skiers climbing up from the highway and skiers from Snowbird are taking responsibility for their own safety and making the climb from the top of the Gad 2 Lift and skiing the long, concave bowls and the steep, rock-shrouded gullies of White Pine. Some feel that lifts and development in White Pine would mean sharing the powder with thousands of skiers, snowcats, and more regulations. Others are convinced that the natural areas of Little Cottonwood Canyon are an unrivaled asset and should remain and continue to add character to this splendid place.

Aerial view toward Snowbird from northeast. Note top of Snowbird tram on ridge at lower center. Gad Valley is to the right of the tram. Contested White Pine Canyon is adjacent to Gad Valley. Lone Peak Wilderness Area at upper right, Mt. Timpanogos, Utah Lake, and Utah Valley are in the background.
Pete Houdeshel

FINDING POWDER

Finding powder has a lot to do with finding sources of information. It helps to know about the storms that produce the snow and where and when it will be softest and deepest. But it is also important to know the people who know about snow and who are willing to share. Junior Bounous may be the best source of all. I called him to ask what he would say to people about finding powder at Snowbird.

"I would encourage them to take a powder lesson," he said without hesitation, as if he had been asked this question many times before. "Our instructors are prepared not only to teach people how to ski powder, but where to find it."

These lessons apparently become a combination of powder skiing and powder finding. I decided to try one. We made the arrangements, and I showed up on a cold, sunny morning, excited about the chance to ski with Junior Bounous.

The first thing I learned is that you don't just pass the time on the tram ride, especially on the day after a significant storm. You scan the slopes for untracked snow. While he was looking, Junior assessed my experience in powder. I told him I had taught myself by watching others and felt comfortable in deep snow. I also told him I would like him to start at square one. So he did. I became the beginner. We clipped into our skis and pushed off along the Cirque Traverse and down Chips Run. Junior stopped part way and told me to follow him off the trail. Together we entered the powder.

"Use your senses," he told me. "Listen to what I tell you, watch what I do, and remem-

Junior Bounous
Scott Nelson, Courtesy of Snowbird

ber how the snow feels." I pushed off in a straight line, skis evenly weighted. I felt the essence of being in, rather than on, the snow as it countered my momentum.

"Keep your body loose," he told me. "A loose body is free of fear." He talked in a low voice, slowly, making certain I understood. He then took me back in my development to a place where I felt secure and comfortable on packed runs. He talked me through a slow uphill turn, a stem turn, then two stems linked together. With each step, he watched to see that I was in control. He explained that control breeds confidence, and confidence helps break down the mystique about powder snow that intimidates people.

It is not new to Junior to be teaching stem turns in powder snow. "I started teaching skiing at Alta back in the forties when everyone learned to ski in the powder. There was no such thing as a groomed slope," he told me.

An important step in beginning to learn powder skiing is the powder christie. Junior showed me how to begin a right turn by stemming. Then, when my shoulders were facing directly down the fall line, he had me pick up my right ski and place it next to the left to complete the turn.

When it was time to assess what I had learned, Junior had a longer and slightly steeper slope that ended on a packed run. We set a goal for five turns.

"Don't worry if all your turns aren't perfect," he said.

As I went through the motions of five powder christies, my mind wandered to the sensation of the snow, soft against my

legs. I felt the even resistance encouraging my balance.

The next and perhaps the most important step is unweighting. For this, Junior reminded me of the difference between unweighting and weight transfer. Transfer of weight from one ski to the next causes the skier to turn, but the unweighted ski is like an undisciplined child and will get into trouble. With proper unweighting, both skis act as one. We talked about how the speed necessary for unweighting is faster than some feel comfortable with. The idea is to weight the skis just enough to check the speed before beginning the next turn, not to stop completely.

Making shorter, sharper turns requires perfect body position. By pulling on me from different angles, Junior simulated the forces that would act on me during a turn: the force of gravity, the resistance of the snow, and my individual tendencies. I became a physics problem, impossible to calculate. The right feel is the only proof.

Junior led me along catwalks to a grove of perfectly spaced trees on the ridge that separates Snowbird from Alta. Following Junior I was able to see the deftness he had developed, ducking low branches, sidestepping rock outcroppings. Each time I caught up with Junior, he was perched with his weight supported by his right ski, placed perpendicular to the fall line, with his other ski pointing ahead on top of the snow. He could be sitting in a custom-made chair. I was beginning to sense decorum.

There came a time, toward the midpoint of the lesson, when I became my own teach-

er. I could feel whether each turn was right or not. Did my chest suck my knees up? Did I land on a platform built by both skis equally? Or did one ski go asunder, forcing my entire body to salvage the turn? Good skiing, I found, is often asking the right questions.

On most runs, Junior insisted that I go first. But there were times when something came over him and he forgot that this was his business and I was his client. It was hard to know whether it was the force of gravity or a sudden passion that made him leap into the fall line and in an effortless string of perfect turns wind his way to the bottom.

Perhaps the most valuable part of the day was the chance to watch Junior ski toward me. I saw how his body refused to raise or lower an inch, and the hill appeared to be moving beneath him. I watched his knees vibrate with the consistency of a sewing machine. I was also able to discern his face as it passed through its different expressions: first, a look of concentration while he got into his rhythm; then the smile when the snow and turning had taken over. When he got close to the bottom of the run, he would grin uncontrollably.

I felt something as I watched Junior ski. It is the same feeling I have when I watch Larry Bird with a basketball or Godinov do a balletic leap. I was seeing the best.

When we finished, I had learned a lot about where to look for powder and what to do once I found it. But more than anything else, I had learned what is possible with proper training and technique.

EARL MILLER

Earl Miller
Courtesy Miller Ski Company

One February, ten years ago, a man was sitting inside one of the lodges at Alta, eating his lunch. Another man approached and asked why he had his skis with him.

"Look, I've almost lost them twice to ski thieves and they're the best skis I've ever had and I don't want to try and replace them."

"They look pretty funny to me," the other man quipped.

"Hey, buddy," the first man said with gritted teeth and a clenched fist as if the insult had been aimed at his mother.

Before things got out of hand, the second man decided to introduce himself. "I'm Earl Miller and I designed those skis."

The skis were Miller Softs, and the owner was typical of those holding title to these magic skis. Earl Miller makes them special—especially for the Rocky Mountains where he has been skiing for over forty years.

It all began in the mid-1960s when Miller was talking with Gene Huber, local skier and owner of the Deep Powder House specialty shop at Alta.

"You make a ski for the kind of powder we get here and I'll sell a thousand pairs," Huber challenged.

Miller was amazed. "You could sell a thousand pairs? Keep talking!"

They did and the next year the Miller Soft was on the market, replacing the Head Deep Powder as the ski for the Wasatch.

The process was exciting for Miller, whose company had been involved in the ski industry as a manufacturer since 1946, the oldest in America. He knew skis, and his engineering and inventing background made the technical part flow. Miller also had the right people helping him—Ted Johnson, Junior Bounous, and Eddie Morris, the best powder skiers in the world.

"We're inland here," Miller says, "and Alta is a big bowl at the top of a steep canyon," his hands showing me just how big the bowl is. "The storms get caught there and swirl around and around and lay down tons of snow. In the past, all this snow was really a nuisance because the people didn't

know how to ski it." But things have changed. "Nowadays, powder skiing is the most esoteric sport there is. Some people will go anywhere and pay any price. Those people buy my skis."

This year, Miller will sell a thousand pairs of his Softs to helicopter skiers (fifty to eighty percent of those taking helicopter trips will be using them), to snow rangers all over the western U.S. and as far away as Argentina and Europe, and many other professional skiers who need a separate ski made for unpacked snow.

"So, what makes the Miller Soft perform so well in Utah's powder?" I ask.

"Part of it is a secret," he says, knowing I would feel cheated if he didn't say that. "The rest is obvious."

He stepped out of the room and came back with the flaming orange ski. Then his hands did most of the talking.

"They are a wide ski, providing lift in lighter snow, characteristic of the Rocky Mountains. They have the side cut of a slalom ski for quicker turning. They have "totality in flex," meaning they flex smoothly throughout their

entire length. The thin cross-section enables the skier not only to cut through untracked snow but also slice. And they are light, six pounds four ounces a pair," he says, handing the ski over the desk to me.

Miller still uses his skis for pleasure in Alta's wide open areas. "I don't do those little, safe turns we used to call chicken turns. I like making fast, wide turns above timber line, throwing up rooster tails. The chicken turn has all but eliminated those glorious falls." He stretched out the word "glorious."

I bought some Miller Softs early in 1986. At first I felt that my reasoning walked the fine line between rationalization and guilt; I didn't need another pair of skis. Once I used them, however, I didn't know how I'd skied so long without them.

Earl Miller is a perfect example of pervading passion. Powder skiing first worked its way into his spare time; then it invaded his business; now it controls his life. But it works for him. If you don't believe me, take your ski rack and your checkbook and go talk to him.

You have probably heard the Brighton Ski Area described as "quaint," as "the place where Salt Lake learns to ski," and as "skiing the way it used to be." What, exactly, do people mean when they use these phrases? I have some ideas.

Quaint. Cute, old-fashioned, slightly curious. At Brighton, cute means no high-rise condominiums, tramways, or outdoor tubs. Old-fashioned is price—$10.00 for a day pass (half that Monday through Thursday). It is more than slightly puzzling how Brighton manages to stay in business in these times of high-tech skiing, with modern money competing for a piece of the fastest growing sport in America.

Where Salt Lake learns to ski. True, there are some very easy runs at Brighton, but the statement may have more to do with Brighton taking pride in *not* being a destination resort. This means that a lot of local people go to Brighton so they don't have to deal with the bussed hoards from every ski club in America, who go somewhere else because all the rooms available wouldn't hold much more than a bus load of people.

Skiing the way it used to be, and possibly the way skiing will have to be in the future if the sport can survive all the hype and liability pressure. Owner Zane Doyle and his sons, Randy and Mike, and manager Gi

Brighton "Kinderski"
Gil Jensen, *Courtesy of Brighton Ski Bowl*

Mount Millicent, Brighton Ski Bowl
Brooke Williams

Jensen are doing all they can to live up to what appears to be an agreement the original owners made with the mountain. Perhaps someone asked very politely if he could use the mountain if he promised to be careful and respectful. Whatever the cause, the result is a feeling that the lifts were built only to provide access to an incredibly wild and diverse alpine terrain. The mountain has remained free to express its personality. And, yes, you can still smell grease from the broiling Brighton burgers at the bottom of the lift and sip ice-cold water from a pipe at the end of every run.

While it may appear that the developers have played down off-the-mountain life, it does exist. The Brighton Lodge has beds for fifty people. If they're full, try down the road at the Brighton Chalets or the Silver Fork Lodge. You can leave your brown bag home and sample the food at the Alpine Rose, the Brighton Manor, or the Chalet at the bottom of Evergreen. For dinner—French country cooking, no less—go into the Brighton Store, walk to the back as if you were looking for the bathroom, go up the stairs, and knock three times. On certain nights (Thursday through Sunday, I think) you will be admitted to the Blind Miner, where Don Despain will personally cook for you.

But the reason that people go to Brighton is to ski. For powder skiing, I pick Brighton because of the freedom I feel there. Riding the Millicent Lift, I think about the role this resort plays as a starting point for an experience of my own making, rather than as entertainment controlled by an army of orange signs and rolls of red rope.

From the top of the lift, I can see for miles. It is time to make a choice. I could ski the named runs, and have done so when the snow was soft and deep. To the west, a traverse leads to the Scree and Lone Pine runs, which are never groomed. If I felt energetic, I could hoist my skis to my shoulder and kick steps up the wind-pocked ridge to ski the face of Mount Millicent. Or I could keep going and climb all the way to the bowls of Wolverine, a peak that sits like a white king, ruling over the area. Today I choose to traverse back toward Twin Lakes Pass, past the sign telling me I am leaving the area and am responsible for myself. I follow a fresh track left by two skiers.

When I catch up with them, we decide to ski the long bowl facing us in the distance. After twenty minutes, the traverse ends and we stand facing a copse of wind-dwarfed trees. We are looking for the space we know is there, like the placket in a woman's skirt, leading to the untouched beauty of knee-deep snow. We slip through the opening, one at a time, and slide smoothly across the flats whose far edge is the beginning of the run. Before pushing off, I take three deep breaths: one to relax, one to adjust my instincts, and one to start the rhythm that my legs will continue. I nudge the hill and gravity takes over. The snow is deep, and my trip to the bottom stirs up thirty small storms.

The Snake Creek Lift, which opened in 1984, adds a new dimension to the resort. I had scorned the possibility of developing such a pristine backcountry area, but I now believe that the world is better off with more people enjoying the beauty of the Snake Creek side of Brighton. Besides, the powdery flanks of Clayton Peak are only moments from the top of the lift. One wrong turn on the Sunshine Run will put you on your way to Heber City, but the forty turns in untracked snow will make the climb back bearable. Many of the runs that are accessible from the Snake Creek Lift are not groomed by machine, so that days after a storm skiers are still bouncing through foamlike crud.

Dependability may be the best trait a ski resort can have. Brighton is so dependable you can set your calendar by it. When the lifts open at Brighton, it's winter. When they close, it's spring. And in-between is all the skiing anyone could ask for.

BRIGHTON INFORMATION

The Skiing. Brighton offers skiing "the way it used to be," according to promotional literature. The area is not a destination resort and is used mostly by locals. Brighton provides skiers with basic needs plus incredible alpine terrain. The forty-three designated trails (twenty-six percent beginner, forty-four percent intermediate, thirty percent advanced) are only part of it. The people who run Brighton seem to pride themselves in letting the personality of the mountains come through, which heightens the spirit of adventure. This means you can find ungroomed bowls, nicely spaced trees, and spectacular views.

The Facility. Four double chair lifts and one triple, night skiing, five restaurants within a mile, four lodges, and no condos. The ski school is PSIA certified and has a staff of sixty instructors.

Location. Twenty-eight miles southeast of Salt Lake City, thirty-three miles from the airport, ten miles up Big Cottonwood Canyon on State Highway 152.

Annual Snowfall. 430 inches.

Season. Two days after the first major snowstorm to whenever people quit coming.

SOLITUDE

I first set eyes on Honeycomb Canyon in 1974. Solitude had been closed that winter during a major transfer of ownership. One day a friend and I decided to ski from Brighton to Solitude and see what Powderhorn was like in the middle of a winter when no one had skied it. The most direct route seemed to be across the Twin Lakes Dam and up what is now the Solbright Trail to a pass on Solitude's main ridge. The plan was to traverse the ridge from the pass, eventually ending at the top of the Powderhorn Lift. We never made it. At the pass, we were hypnotized by the huge face of the Honeycomb Cliffs. The cliffs stretched out to our right, curving slightly, like a giant outdoor movie screen. Without much talk, we made a new plan: we would ski Honeycomb Canyon. We cautiously made our way through the trees, skiing the adequate openings one after another until time ran out.

I skied in this magical place often during the next three years. I learned Honeycomb's moods. I knew where to ski when slides were possible and where to find powder after a week of sun. I knew about those rare

days when conditions allowed a long traverse under the cliffs. I would never forget the spectacular runs that followed.

In 1977 three California businessmen bought Solitude. Convinced that antiquated equipment and inept management were the main causes for Solitude's problems, they embarked on a twenty-year turnabout. During the first years of new ownership, the only difference I noticed was skiers leaking out of the resort and down into my Honeycomb Canyon.

The ensuing years brought more and more people into the canyon—cross-country skiers in from the top as well as downhill skiers from Solitude. Still, there was always untracked snow to play in. In 1982 Solitude had a big year. New runs were cut and the Summit Lift was built, expanding the resort boundaries into Honeycomb Canyon. When I went back to Honeycomb after a four-year absence in January 1986, I sorted through my memory and decided that the Powderhorn Lift would give me the best run into the canyon. My mind played over each day I had spent in Honeycomb—the thrills

and spills, the times when the snow was so light that my imagination had me dancing on clouds. Thoughts of reunion lifted me.

My excitement was short-lived. As I approached the unloading point, a sign on the operator's shelter announced that Honeycomb was closed. I was not surprised, many skiers had warned me about this possibility. Since I could see no reason to close the canyon, I was confident that it would be open before I quit for the day. I would be patient.

For two runs I was content to ski the powder that remained between runs off the Powderhorn Lift. I crossed over and rode the Inspiration Lift with a ski patrolman who had heard the Canyon was open. If he could arrange it, he would ski it with me. Honeycomb was closed from this side, too. The patrolman explained that the canyon was open over eighty percent of the time, but usually from the Summit Lift. I took the quickest route I knew to the Sunrise Lift, then down Deer Trail to the bottom of Summit. As I rode up again I was beginning to feel a bit frustrated, wondering about the merits

Left: Solitude Ski Area and the Honeycomb Cliffs
Chris Noble

Right
John Barstow

of resort expansion.

I was relieved to see the temporary, red "open" board hanging on the Honeycomb sign. I skated off the ramp and over to the edge of the canyon and looked over. There they were, the Honeycomb Cliffs. There was a faint familiarity in the wind that bit at my fingers while I tightened my boots.

I stood there for a while, looking out across the snow. My view was interrupted by ropes that had been placed to guide skiers down the correct path to the bottom of the canyon. A row of ropes and "closed" signs bisected the upper part of the canyon. I mounted the ridge and climbed as fast as my cumbersome equipment would allow. In twenty minutes I reached the top of a run I recognized very well. It began as a huge bowl, pitched at twenty-five degrees. Then it tapered and fell steeply into the bottom of the canyon. Only a few skiers had been here. As I pushed off and began to turn, the weight of my frustration eased. Just before dropping into the stream that runs along the bottom of the canyon, I stopped, as I had done many times in the past. If this particular slope were to slide, it would happen here where the slope angle changes. Looking carefully for cracks and signs of settling, I saw only the packed and bumpy surface of the well-used run below me.

As I joined the main run down the center of the canyon, I thought about the adventure that once brewed in this place. The wildness had gone out of it. Honeycomb Canyon had changed. My reunion had become a requiem.

"Solitude has some of the best snow safety people in the business," says Rick Wyatt, who works avalanche control for the Utah State Highway Department. "They have impeccable judgment and the confidence of the resort owners who don't pressure them into keeping Honeycomb open. It may have been better to leave it for the tourers."

It comes down to the fine line of judgment between backcountry skiers who are responsible only for their own safety and snow-safety people who are responsible for hundreds. It is not as if backcountry skiers are safer with Honeycomb being off-limits—I don't think anyone was killed there before.

But snow rangers get paid to act on their better judgment. No one can fault them for that. What it comes down to is that lifts are sometimes added not so much to enhance the skier's experience, but to increase the numbers of skiers on the mountain at one time which means more money for the resort.

Solitude is a valuable example of what happens when ski areas expand. Skiers and others who use and love the mountains will always be fettered with the decision of how to respond to plans for bigger resorts. On the one hand expansion means a broadened ski experience, with new terrain to attract more of the money spent on skiing. On the other hand, in a limited environment, when one thing expands, another contracts. When a resort in the Wasatch Mountains expands, a wild place contracts. It is time to decide if we need more domestic skiing or more places in which to run wild.

SOLITUDE INFORMATION

The Skiing. Solitude's boundary surrounds 1,000 acres which are nicely divided between open bowls, tree-lined runs, and ungroomed forest. The area provides terrain for skiers of any ability. **The Facility.** Five lifts serve 2,000 vertical feet of skiing. Three of the lifts end at a ridge overlooking Honeycomb Canyon with a spectacular view of the Honeycomb Cliffs. There are two slope side restaurants, and the Main Lodge houses a cafeteria, Houlihan's Bar and Grill, and a newly redecorated lounge. **Location.** Two miles below Brighton in Big Cottonwood Canyon. **Annual Snowfall.** 410 inches. **Season.** Late November to mid-April.

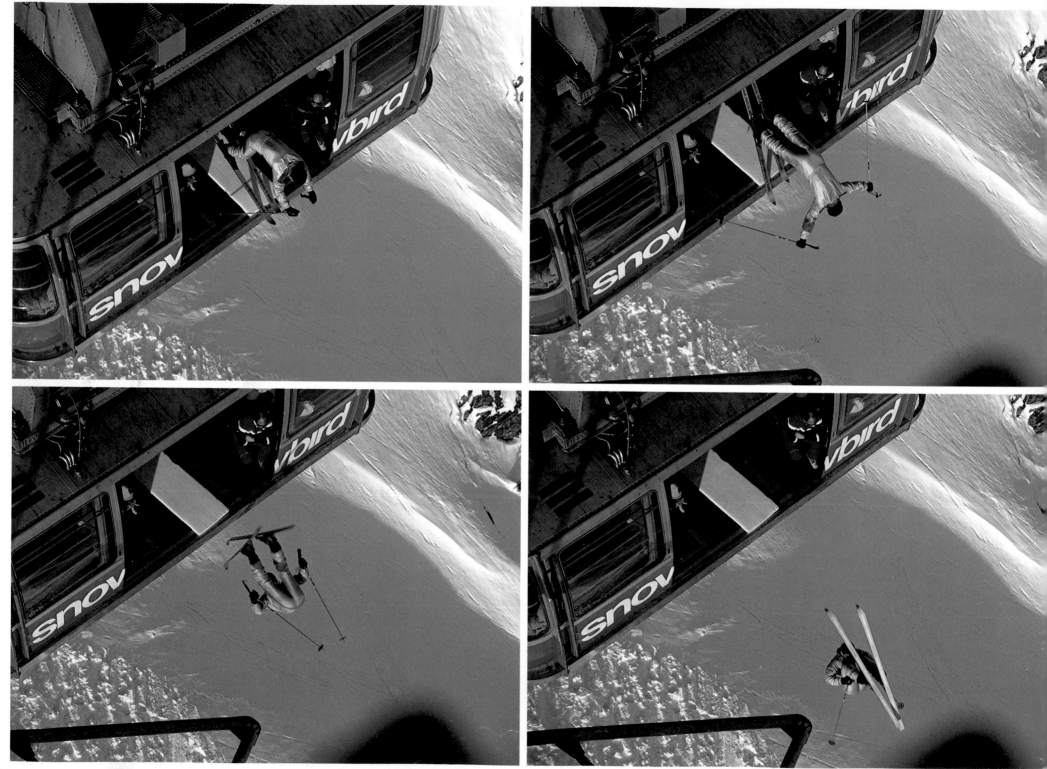

SKI PASS

You can't ski at a resort without a ski pass. After paying as little as $5 or as much as $30 for one, you stick it to the wire triangle connected to your parka or pants and forget about it. Had you looked closely at your pass, you would have seen that it contained a code telling the lift attendant if the day you bought it for is the day you are using it. Then, in small print, is this notice:

The purchaser and user of this ticket assumes and understands that skiing is a hazardous sport, that bare spots, variations in snow, ice, and terrain along with bumps, moguls, stumps, forest growth and debris and rocks and many other hazards or obstacles exist within this ski area. In using the ticket and skiing at the area, such dangers are recognized and accepted whether they are marked or unmarked. The skier realizes that falls and collisions do occur and injuries may result, and therefore assumes the burden of skiing under control at all times.

Unfortunately for the sport, the waiver doesn't mean much. Even though the number of skiers who are injured is decreasing, the amount that resorts are required to pay for liability insurance is exploding. For the 1985-1986 season, resorts received bills reflecting increases of from thirty to one hundred percent. The reason for the increase is simple: attorneys do not consider skiing a risk sport and insurance companies, smarting from personal injury suits, are refusing to take a chance. The immediate result will be higher ticket prices. The long-range costs are uncertain, but one result may be that resorts will choose to provide entertainment for their customers rather than experience.

"The main problem," according to Junior Bounous of Snowbird, "is speed." Junior remembers when the ski resort had no control over the mountain. Their main responsibility was to keep the lift running and possibly serve chile. He also remembers a day, over thirty years ago, when the snow was so terrible that the Deseret News Ski School was about to be cancelled. "I had to do something," Junior recalls, "so I got a snowcat we had to get into some of the cabins and used it to pack out the entire slope." He had no idea how this simple action would change resort skiing.

The economics of the sport now require resorts to groom more and more of their runs to compete for the money spent on skiing. "We've got a tiger by the tail," says Junior. "Better machines are being designed to groom steeper terrain which encourages skiers to ski at speeds which are unsafe."

The serious injuries occur when speeding skiers lose control and hit trees, lift towers, buildings, or other skiers. Regardless of the circumstances, skiers who sustain a permanent injury expect compensation. They sue.

Should resort owners be required to guarantee the safety of skiers who pay to use their facilities? Are they responsible for providing a playground, insulated from the real world, or merely access to the great beyond, where those who enter do so with the knowledge that the environment is wild and demands respect? Should ski area owners try to eliminate all risk, or should we begin to look at risk in a different way? Is it time to realize that risk in the proper amounts can enhance our existence, and that eliminating it would sand away the sharp edges that remind us we are really alive?

Stewart Aitchison

PARKWEST INFORMATION

The Skiing. First-time visitors to Park-West who stand at the base of the resort might wonder if perhaps they have misinterpreted reports of the area, as only the wide-open beginner slopes are visible. But the majority of the resort is tucked away into four canyons that must be skied to be appreciated. Intermediates can choose from wide, tree-lined trails winding two and a half miles down the mountain or test their ability on some of the resort's notable mogul runs. ParkWest has a fine mix of open bowls, powder chutes, or long, steep, fall line runs to challenge the expert. There is also an abundance of off-trail skiing. Of the forty-six runs, twenty-one are advanced, fourteen are intermediate, and eleven are easy.

The Facility. Seven chair lifts serve the 2,200-foot vertical drop and can carry 6,700 skiers per hour. ParkWest offers lessons by the Professional Ski Instructors of America as well as nordic downhill lessons for those who want to learn the telemark turn. And a new program for the 1985-1986 season, Centered Skiing, helps the advanced or strong intermediate with personal, specific problems. Three mountain restaurants offer a selection of dining possibilities.
Location. Twenty-six miles east of Salt Lake via I-80, four miles south on U-224 at the Park City exit.
Annual Snowfall. 300 inches.
Season. Early December to early April.

TREE SKIING

To ski the trees you need precise planning, razor-edged technique, and a flair for surprise. Trees add a major dimension to powder skiing. Unlike skiing open bowls, tree skiing requires you to react to the rhythm of the forest.

"Go slow," according to Eddie Morris, who has spent the past thirty-five years as a ski instructor in the Wasatch Mountains. This is the best advice for those intent on learning the nuances of tree skiing. "The leg action is important, as there is no time to unweight. The smooth rolling of the knees, side to side, and a quiet upper body are essential." Watch the spaces between the trees, because watching the tree can be magnetic, bonding you to it literally. Any speed at all will transform the friendly fir into ironwood.

When I ski in the trees, I feel as if I am being put to a test. The trees seem to play with me, causing me to kickturn and duck, grabbing and pulling at anything loose and nonessential. Then, more times than not, the spaces will widen, matching my turns. The rhythm the trees have picked for me becomes my own. It feels as though I am catching up with the wind.

Skiing the trees
Chris Noble

PARKWEST

It was January, a month known for the fog that covers the Salt Lake Valley like a wet, dirty, down quilt. It sits here for weeks, held down by persistent high pressure. The result is depressing, murky air in the city and early spring in the mountains, where high temperatures and constant sunlight make powder a memory.

Unable to work, I had been staring out the window for hours when the phone rang. "Do you want to ski some powder?" It was Tom Smart and I thought he was kidding.

"Where, in Canada?" I replied.

"Trust me."

My spirits lifted as I drove over Parley's Summit and emerged from the fog into painful sunlight. I picked Tom up at his home in Pinebrook, halfway between Salt Lake and ParkWest, and we sped down the wet,

steaming roads. In a few minutes we were at ParkWest. Two lift rides and a short traverse put us at the base of Murdock Peak. Crossing the area boundary, we began kicking steps up the ridge to the summit. I was still not convinced that there was any powder to be found, here or anywhere in the Wasatch Mountains. The rocks were dripping with melting ice, and the settled snow made climbing the ridge easy. Within ten minutes we were standing on top and things began to look up. A long protected bowl stretched out beneath us. It was lined on the east and west by large conifers, and the sun's southern path kept its north face shaded.

The old snow had settled to about four inches deep on top of a firm base. It was light enough to surpass any of my expectations, but it looked tricky. I knew it was lying there,

piled up like deflated ghosts ready to leap up at any moment and scare the hell out of us. I timidly eased into the fall line and found that turning required exaggerated unweighting, precise edging, and more concentration than in normal conditions. The conditions weren't bad enough to keep us from skiing this hill three times.

The light began to fade just as we finished our last run and headed for Pinebrook, the back way. "I was born for this," I thought as we moved out single file and made a turn down the wrong drainage. We wallowed in the dark for two hours in hip-deep death crud. Eventually, we emerged onto I-80 five miles off target.

There is always a price.

PARK CITY

Park City is full of contrasts. Developers have worked hard to provide visitors with modern conveniences in a setting that commemorates the late 1800s when mining was king. Historic Main Street and the old mining buildings dotting the ski slopes provide some insight into a life-style that was perhaps more colorful than the one that has replaced it.

Miners worked hard. They spent ten hours a day underground, breathing air laced with dust, the residue of rocks broken by the continual swinging of heavy sledge hammers. The miners were always soaked to the bone by the water that flowed constantly in the mine. Most days ended with a long, uncomfortable train ride to the mouth of the mine. The only thing to look forward to was a warm shower, a bowl of stew, and stale bread before falling into a hard bunk, only to arise in time to make the next shift.

Paydays kept them going. Twice each month the train rides were raucous affairs, with the men bantering, scheming, and dreaming about what would transpire during the hours before the next bell signaled another day of work. Work-worn bodies were camouflaged by light-footed dances into the boarding houses, where miners were transformed into eligible men ready to take on whatever the night served up.

What followed was a collage of expression and activity. At that time, Park City had as many saloons as there are condominium complexes today. The miners would drink and bet. Arm wrestling would make way for fistfighting. When all the egos had been either boosted or burst, the men would make their way to a row of tidy little houses on Heber Avenue, where they would finish the night and their money with one of Mother Urban's girls.

Mother Urban was the first hostess of Park City. Weighing in at two hundred pounds, she walked on a wooden leg and had a foul-beaked parrot perched on her shoulder. In addition to clean and affectionate ladies, Mother Urban was famous for her charitable donations and chicken soup. She was appreciated by both the men working the mines and their superiors. Without Mother Urban and her girls, the miners would have left town to fulfill basic needs and they might not have returned for three or four days.

Park City's hosts still serve up a delicacy that many would spend their last dollar on: powder snow. While it may not replace Mother Urban's girls, for many, a constant source of powder is not a luxury, it is a necessity. More than one person has designated the act of rhythmically flowing through untracked powder on skis a close second on

Park City
Patrick McDowell

the list of life's most important activities.

Gino Boyle runs the Park City Host Program. He and his seven hosts and hostesses are responsible for seeing that skiers are shown the best possible experience while they are in Park City. The program was designed to give visitors tours of the mountain, matching runs with ability. This eliminates the customary floundering that normally accompanies the first day at a new resort. Gino has seen the host program expand to allow a more personal touch. "It is not unusual," he says, "to have clients request exactly what kind of skiing they want to do." After a test run to determine the client's ability, the host becomes a personal guide. This allows powder skiers who are unfamiliar with Park City to call (two weeks in advance, please) and make arrangements for a host to show them the other side of the resort.

Jupiter Bowl is a must. Since a lift was built here a few years ago, this area has become famous for its powder skiing. Riding up the Pioneer Lift, the area served by the Jupiter Lift spreads out in front of you. On your left are McConkey's Bowl and Puma Bowl. Across and to your right are steep chutes in the trees and exciting ridges. To the far right is the immense Scott's Bowl. It is not readily apparent how to get to all these places. Some

require short hikes, others, long traverses with minor maneuvers only Park City veterans know. Your host will get you to the place you want to ski.

The tree skiing in Jupiter Bowl is stupendous. You have nothing to lose by telling your host that your Park City experience would be greatly enhanced by just one afternoon of untracked skiing in the trees.

The Host Program at Park City is a grand idea, and it has great potential. I can see the possibility of the program including experienced mountain guides to take clients beyond the resort boundaries. Park City is a perfect place to initiate this. There is unlimited powder skiing within reasonable distances from lift tops, and while the potential for avalanches exists, there are safe routes that can be used in any conditions. In the European tradition, this *off piste* skiing would soon gain popularity among powder skiers seeking a more reliable source of their favorite substance.

The Park City Host Program succeeds by offering insight into everything that the largest resort in Utah has to offer. The hosts' personal touch and attention to individual requests and requirements make this program unique. With your own Park City host, almost anything is possible.

PARK CITY INFORMATION

The Skiing. Park City offers skiers of any ability all the skiing they could ever want. Beginners and novices have their own area, served by two chair lifts, First Time and Three Kings. If they want to ride the gondola, they can ski the Meadow and Claimjumper runs to the Prospector Lift, or they can try Webster to the Pioneer run. Intermediates can ride the King Con triple chair lift, which begins in the bottom of Thayne's Canyon and provides unlimited, wide runs at a perfect angle. The Prospector chair provides access to the popular Hidden Splendor, Sitka, Powder Keg, Payday, and Parley's Park runs. The Pioneer Lift is off the beaten path and gives skiers the early morning sun. The experts have Blue Slip Bowl, the Hoist, the U.S. Ski Team runs, Silver Skis, Double Jack, Glory Hole, and Silver King. Jupiter Bowl has wide, steep, open faces, chutes, gullies, and cliffs as well as some of the best glade skiing available at any resort. The skiing in Puma and McConkey's Bowl makes the hike required well worth it.

Altogether, Park City has eighty-two designated runs and 2,200 acres of open bowl skiing.

The Facility. Eight double chair lifts, five triples, and the longest four-person gondola in the West provide skiing for almost 19,000 skiers every hour. The base of the new Town Lift is just one block from the bottom of historic Main Street and gives skiers a separate access to the area. There is night skiing on Payday, the longest, lighted run in the Rockies.

Location. Twenty-seven miles east of Salt Lake City via six-lane Interstate 80 and U-224.

Annual Snowfall. 350 inches.

Season. Mid-November to mid-April.

Left above: Deer Valley
James Kay

Right above: Stein Erickson
Lodge, Deer Valley
James Kay

Left below: ''Ballroom skiing''
at Deer Valley
Chris Noble

Right below: Snowpark Lodge,
midway at Deer Valley
Chris Noble

By the time I took my first trip to Deer Valley, it had been open for six years. During that period I had learned a lot about this resort of resorts. I had read articles in *Skiing* and *Gourmet*. I had seen pictures and heard stories. When I finally loaded up all my expectations and packed the best outfit I could borrow, I was ready. Something in the back of my mind told me there was more to know.

By noon on that first day, I was progressing nicely in checking off my preconceptions. I had met many of the color-coded employees (green for service, red for patrol, and green and white for instruction) who acted as if they were there to do a job, not just waiting for the time to ski. I found that this attitude of service-with-a-style is part of everything skiers require of a resort.

I had wandered in and out of lodges built to withstand the pressures not only of many winters and tons of snow but also of the ever-changing architectural ideals. The atmosphere was rich and warm all at once. And not once on five rides on four different chairlifts had I been banged in the calves, jerked to a stop, pushed down an off-ramp, or forced to wait in a line. The runs I had skied were immaculate and exciting. Somehow they are able to groom runs at Deer Valley at a greater pitch than I had seen before. I was also pleasantly surprised to find runs that were not groomed. The recent opening of the May-

flower area adds some challenging terrain, much of it tamed only by adventurous skiers.

I had reserved my greatest expectations for the food. Comments like "the food alone is worth the trip" and "this is the best food above seven thousand feet anywhere in the country, if not the world" had primed my pallet. My meager budget forced me to look for a cafeteria, and I was directed to the Huggery where people do serve themselves on trays. But there the association with any other cafeteria ends. At the natural buffet, fruits, vegetables, salads, and breads were piled so high I could scarcely see over them. I stacked as much as I could on one plate and found a seat. A pasta salad with peppers and long cuts of beef was the best I had had above—or below—seven thousand feet.

After lunch, the weather became unpredictable, with fits of fog and wind and blowing snow. The descriptions of Deer Valley had led me to believe that any unpleasant weather came at night when no one would be bothered. I slipped into the trees off the side of the Sterling Lift. The scent of the conifers and the tapping of a lone chickadee hung in the wind-protected stillness. There was powder—although only four inches on an unpredictable base, hardened by three stormless weeks. Skiing here would be a challenge. I eased into my first turn and quickly learned that each

linked turn required a leap of faith to check speed and change directions fast enough to stay within the limited spaces. Four turns through the first opening, I misjudged a critical distance and hit a small aspen. The sounds, first of bone hitting wood, then of the squeaking groan an aspen makes when it bends, were all I remember. Pain exploded in my right knee. After a few minutes, the pain eased long enough for me to be aware that I was alone. The setting that had attracted me suddenly held me captive. No one had seen me fall, and no matter how uncommonly civilized Deer Valley was, I was alone, injured on the side of a wild and spirited mountain. As I stood to assess the damage, a ground blizzard purled around my feet. Fortunately, my movement was impaired by a bruise rather than a break. A few flexes and extensions made me confident that I could ski away from this mishap. I was lucky.

In the mountains, a glint of sun can warm you; you can hear birds or catch a glimpse of an ermine diving through the snow. A mountain can hold you and caress you and change your mind, or its wildness can rear up and throw off its trappings. It can squeeze until you cannot yell and break your bones like twigs. You can never tell. The mountains of Deer Valley are no different.

DEER VALLEY INFORMATION

The Skiing. "The class act of skiing," according to most who have skied there, Deer Valley boasts forty-two runs on two mountains: Bald Eagle at 8,400 feet and Bald at 9,400 feet. Fifteen percent of the runs are rated as easy, fifty percent are more difficult and thirty-five percent are most difficult. Much effort is spent by the Deer Valley staff to ensure skiers the runs are in perfect condition every day. Most of the resort's runs are cut directly down the fall line and groomed constantly by the latest in equipment. According to the press packet, "such unpleasant surprises as moguls, ruts, and icy patches are virtually eliminated." In 1985 the addition of the Clipper Chair increased the resort by sixty-one acres, most of it serving advanced skiers.

The Facility. Seven triple chairs and one double provide access to 2,200 vertical feet. An added benefit is snow making equipment on 4.5 miles of trails. Deer Valley provides the latest in ski instruction, using the American Teaching Method. The resort gives skiers the highest quality food, lodging, and service.

Location. Two miles east of the Park City Resort, surrounding the town of Park City.

Annual Snowfall. 300 inches.

Season. Thanksgiving Day to early April.

"This is an art center," marketing man Peter Crowley told me the first time we talked about Sundance. "Robert Redford wants this to be known for the art, not the skiing." The statement didn't do much to fire my enthusiasm. While driving up the canyon east of Provo, I realized that the only times I hear Sundance mentioned are with reference to the art programs, particularly the Sundance Institute for Film Studies. But as I turned onto the Sundance road, the intimacy of the canyon flowed into my car the way it must have the first time Redford visited here on a hunting trip more than two decades ago. In 1961 he bought two acres for $2,500; two years later he built his home here.

Redford, the artist, was very happy here for a few years. He felt secure and free to do his work in an environment as different from his other home in Manhattan as heaven and earth. Aware that developers with other ideas had eyes on the place, he bought four thousand acres in 1968 to keep things the way he liked them.

Redford, the skier, quickly recognized that the terrain was conducive to skiing. The area had the potential for long, wide runs in steep bowls and gentle canyons. Part of the acreage he bought was the old Timp Haven Ski Area, which had a J-bar and a T-bar.

Three miles past the turnoff I pulled into a parking lot. It was so small that I thought I'd made a wrong turn. The surrounding buildings were small, cabin-like, in a constant state of Christmas. They were connected by narrow, partially frozen streams criss-crossed by romantic bridges.

My friends, Chris and Marjie, and I would be staying in a beautiful three-level mountain cabin, owned by a Brigham Young University professor and his family. The house is similar to many which can be rented by traveling skiers. We would eat at the Tree Room, a large space built around a huge tree. We dined like royalty. The food was perfect and the ambience unaffected by fad or fashion. We could have been at a party in Redford's own home. A large, brightly colored Navajo rug covered one wall, and Native American art fit as perfectly in the room as the old tree did. It all had the feel of being carefully collected.

The Tree Room became symbolic of the entire Sundance resort. Redford, with his own personal needs, has guided the progress of this development. Intrusion into the landscape has been minimized by the attitude of one man adhering to his own ideas of how things should be rather than to the potential for profit. My hunch is that the plans for the future will be carried out in a similar manner. Fifty cottages for artists in residence (this is an art center) or destination skiers, and a 150-seat theater and screening room are being planned now. Although relatively new, Sundance seems dug in. It seems to belong.

The next morning, a two-minute walk took us to one of the main runs served by the Mandan Lift. This gave us a chance to warm up on an eggshell-smooth surface before meeting a representative from Sundance who would show us around. At the bottom Rick Black was waiting for us. After one run with this instructor and former free-style skier, I was glad we had a chance to loosen up. Not only is this man a fantastic skier, but he loves adventure. The combination can be disastrous or delightful, depending on how closely you follow and the length of his reins. We spent half the day in developed areas, skiing everything from intermediate runs perfectly pitched and sidewalk smooth, to uninterrupted moguls, big enough to hide children.

The rest of the day Rick gave us a personal tour of places known only to people who have skied Sundance most of their adult lives. The high point came near the end of the day. After giving us a minor warning, Rick took off on a thin, winding track. Marjie and I followed at a safe distance. We rounded the last bend just in time to watch Rick drop into a tuck at the top of a wide, packed run. He picked up speed until just when we thought he would run into the side of Archies Knoll he sat way back and shot like a rocket up the side, coming to a stop one hundred feet up. We cautiously tried the same thing, but our lack of confidence left us short; 1,245 side-steps later, we met on top. The view of Mount Timpanogos was suffocating: flowing ridges in two directions, a towering summit blanketing the entire area with huge, afternoon shadows. The plan was to ski the north side of this perfect knoll together for the benefit of Chris, who had sacrificed this adventure for the chance to take a few good photographs from below. We pushed off in unison. I quickly discovered that the line I had picked was tricky. The snow was hardened by the wind, and the spaces needed more quickness than I had. In three turns, I blew up. I raised up from the hole I had made and chipped the snow from beneath my glasses quickly enough to see Rick disappear into the aspens at the bottom of a perfect set of tracks. Marjie pulled up fast as a small surface slide flowed in from behind her, knee deep. I gathered my scattered equipment and finished my run. As I pulled up to the others, they were snickering. "What's so funny?" I asked, checking to see if I had put something on backwards. Snow was falling from my clothes and piling up around my feet. Rick answered. "I can see you forgot this is an art center."

Mount Timpanogos from Sundance
Chris Noble

49

To a geologist, the mountains east of Ogden are complex. A number of eastward-moving thrust faults have piled plates indiscriminately, reminiscent of fast-moving freight cars piling into a wall. Scientists are still trying to find some order. On the north side of Ogden Canyon near the Pineview Reservoir is a textbook example of a folding thrust fault.

Ogden Canyon is a transition between two valleys. To the west is the city of Ogden, with thousands of people, cars, trains, businesses, and a college. To the east are a few dozing towns and a lot of pasture. This valley is surrounded by skiing: on the east side, Powder Mountain; to the south, Snowbasin; and in the northwest corner, Nordic Valley. At the Pineview Dam, ten miles east of Ogden, skiers have two choices: they can turn left for Powder Mountain and Nordic Valley or go straight for Snowbasin. It's a hard choice to make, so do what I did. The first day I turned left; the next, I went straight.

Aspens, Beaver Mountain
Jay Krajic

Chris Noble

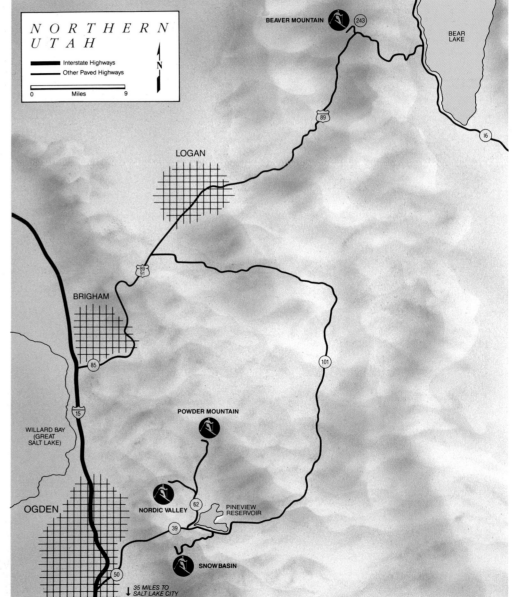

NORTHERN UTAH

Interstate Highways
Other Paved Highways

0   Miles   9

N

BEAVER MOUNTAIN 243
BEAR LAKE
89
16
LOGAN
89 91
BRIGHAM
85
101
15
WILLARD BAY (GREAT SALT LAKE)
POWDER MOUNTAIN
OGDEN
NORDIC VALLEY 62 PINEVIEW RESERVOIR
39
50
SNOWBASIN
↓ 35 MILES TO SALT LAKE CITY

Left: Skiing the aspens
Chris Noble

*Top right: Powder Mountain Ski
Area. Base facilities and
parking area can be seen on
ridge near upper right of photo*
Courtesy of Ski Utah

Below right
James Kay

A ski resort name is usually created to attract eyes scanning promotional literature. Sometimes resorts adopt a catchy geographical place name. Either way, marketing plays a major role. It took a good deal of nerve, however, for Dr. Alvin Cobabe to name his resort Powder Mountain. Like naming a newborn child Einstein, there is a lot to live up to. By the time the resort opened in 1972, Cobabe had been skiing the mountain for nine years. To him, the name was fitting.

"Utah has the greatest snow on earth, and Powder Mountain has the greatest snow in Utah," boasted mountain manager Steve Mathews. How do you argue with someone armed with that kind of confidence? Since I hadn't been there, I couldn't. But I was skeptical. Skiing at Powder Mountain would be satisfying, if not for the enjoyment, for the proof that would give credence to my skepticism.

My day began with a drive up a steep canyon. From the sleepy town of Eden, Utah, the road seems to lunge at the sky. Some say that Powder Mountain is the only ski resort where the road is steeper than the runs. That's not quite true. A few miles past the Wolf Creek condominium development, I started seeing ski tracks on both sides of the canyon. There were skiers waiting on the side of the road for the shuttle to take them back to the resort. As I pulled into the parking lot, I was drooling with the anticipation of skiing the walls of this canyon.

I had made arrangements for a ski patrolman to show me around. Since Powder Mountain doesn't have any guide service, the ski patrol has this responsibility. Bob Finder, five-year veteran of the Powder Mountain Ski Patrol, was waiting at the ski shop. I got right to the point.

"I want to ski powder," I told him.

"That's easy," he said. We took off down the Drifter run to the bottom of the Timberline Lift.

"I don't like to continually brag up this mountain," he told me on the way up, "but we have as much powder skiing as most people can handle." Looking down, I noticed wide-open bowls with only a narrow groomed portion along one side. The rest was marked by the linked S's of powder skiers. The tracks could still be distinguished three days after the last storm. We skied the long open bowls of the Lakeview run in untracked powder. From the top the Great Salt Lake is visible. A short traverse took us to the Hidden Lake Lift.

On the Hidden Lake Lift, we talked about skiing the "backside." Bob informed me that the "backside" had been renamed "Powder Country." The perfect terrain that Powder Mountain is built on has made it possible for each of the three lifts to culminate on the top of its own ridge. Skiers can ski the planned runs on one side, or they can cross over without hiking and ski the powder on the other. It is a perfect setup. The powder runs are long and vary from open bowls to steep tree skiing. They all end about two miles down the canyon from the resort.

From Hidden Lake, there are three main drainages to ski. We picked the first. Bob had noticed that the crest of a small ridge had not been skied, so he quickly found it and together we turned down it, traversing for more. Eventually we ended up in a clearing adjacent to the road. From there, a trail dropped us farther down the canyon where we met four others who had come from another lift. In two minutes, a livestock truck outfitted with a canvas cover, benches, and ski racks came down the canyon to pick us up. In five minutes, we were back at the resort. This shuttle is a great idea. It's free. It's part of Powder Mountain's Powder Country Package.

I questioned Bob about safety in Powder Country. He informed me that avalanche control is necessary not only to keep the skiers safe, but also to keep the road open. After a storm, the patrolmen string out along the ridges on both sides of the canyon, digging pits and testing for stability. They use explosive hand charges when necessary. "The more the area gets skied," he told me, "the less likely there will be any surprises."

The next time off the Hidden Lake Lift, we headed in a different direction to ski Boundary, a new run that was cut to open up an entire area along the southern edge of the resort. The run itself is a thin, groomed, intermediate run. For Bob and me it became an access route to still more untracked bliss. All along the run, there were places to drop off and ski powder. We picked a gentle route through trees, perfectly spaced for novice skiers to test their newly-acquired skills.

Bob and I skied powder all day—another run on Lakeview, the backside of the Timberline Lift, and a different run off Hidden Lake.

Pinnin' and grinnin'; telemark skiing the high country
Chris Noble

POWDER MOUNTAIN INFORMATION

The Skiing. Powder Mountain consists of thirty-one groomed runs covering five hundred acres on three mountains. Ten percent are for beginners, seventy percent for intermediates, and twenty percent are for experts. The resort is laid out so that the back of each of the three mountains can be skied by powder skiers. This adds 2,000 acres of "Powder Country" to the resort's total area.
The Facility. Three lifts and two surface tows can move 4,800 skiers each hour and provide access to 1,300 vertical feet. Skiers using the back side of Powder Mountain will find themselves two miles below the resort when their run is over, where a free shuttle will pick them up and take them back for more. There are three day lodges for quick meals and a restaurant and lounge for more relaxed dining. Lodging is available on the ski slope or at the base of the mountain. Two ski shops serve both downhill and cross-country skiers.
Location. Fifty-five miles north of the Salt Lake International Airport, via I-15 north to Odgen's 12th Street exit, then east nineteen miles through Ogden Canyon.
Annual Snowfall. In excess of 500 inches.
Season. Mid-November to May.

We caught the last shuttle back to the resort just ahead of the patrol who had swept Powder Country, making sure any straggling skiers were safe. Riding back to the resort, I met Jake, an off-duty lift operator looking for adventure. It was 4:00 p.m. and I thought the day was over. Jake had other ideas. The Sundown Lift runs all night for skiing under lights, and we had noticed five sets of beautiful tracks off the high ridge east of the top of the lift. We rode the lift in waning light and began climbing the long, scalloped ridgeline. It was only fair; I had skied powder all day without working for it. In half an hour we were where we needed to be—atop a wide-open shot with nothing but snow and space between us and the parking lot. I pushed off. The trees were no more than dark spots against the perfect snow. I eased into my rhythm and began the longest string of turns I have ever had. I only stopped once to avoid a cliff band that was invisible from the top. As I looked back to check my tracks, I saw that the mountain had become a pure white wall against a darkening sky.

"The greatest snow . . . " What are we really talking about? The amount? The moisture content? Yes, but for a ski resort there is more. Is it easy to get to, and does it last? And my big question—Are powder skiers happy? At Powder Mountain the answer is "yes" all around.

I thought back to that confident resort manager. Before I'd skied Powder Mountain, I didn't feel I could challenge him. When I was through, I wouldn't. A mountain like this should be named Powder.

SNOWBASIN

Since 1977 when Pete Seibert and his partners bought Snowbasin, they have taken a low-key approach to skiing. I hadn't thought much about skiing there until I happened onto one of their brochures. But I know that the resort you read about in promotional literature and the one you ski at aren't necessarily the same. The artist's rendering of Snowbasin exudes adventure. Is this just a good job of advertising, or did the artist have something special to work with? I had to find out.

It's not easy, driving the fifty miles from Salt Lake City, with its canyons laced with so many world-class resorts. Seibert had come all the way from Vail, the resort he started back in the 1960s. Surely I could sacrifice a day. But I knew the deck was stacked in my favor; I had heard about Vail and I doubted a man with Seibert's experience and knowledge about skiing would take a step down.

I had three things to find out: What can Snowbasin offer the skier who defines adventure as more than groomed runs and on-the-hill snacks? How are curious powder skiers treated? How close to reality is the map in the brochure?

Here are my findings. At Snowbasin, what you see is what you ski.

The picture shows considerable open space that is not designated as trail or run. This could mean there is terrain that cannot be skied for reasons impossible to illustrate, such as ground features or pitch. On my first run, I found these "blanks" to be not only skiable but they were also exciting

knolls with open faces. The great thing about these knolls is the climb required to get to the tops. One in particular took only three minutes. I was amazed to find that the six inches of new snow that had fallen the night before was still untracked when I skied it at eleven a.m. This is unheard of in most of the Wasatch.

I won't say that curious powder skiers are encouraged, but almost. The resort boundaries are clearly defined on the map and on the mountain. Skiing the delicious bowls above and beyond the top of Middle Bowl and Porcupine Lifts requires crossing an imaginary line between yellow signs. These signs did not make me feel criminal or suicidal; they simply let me know that the areas I could see beyond—Mt. Ogden, The Needles, DeMoisey Peak, Strawberry Bowl, No Name, and John Paul—were not part of the resort. Leaving the resort was like leaving the schoolyard or the country. The responsibility shifts.

At one point, I joined a group following a high trail off the top of the Middle Bowl Lift. A short traverse put us on the shoulder of DeMoisey Peak at the edge of the resort. After reading the sign, we pushed off into Strawberry Bowl. As I stood in the middle of this huge bowl, I marveled at the wildness of the place. There were no lift towers in sight. The wind blew through the trees and across the open slopes, erasing any evidence that we were not the first.

The skiing in Strawberry Bowl is exciting without being steep. The first drop was

twenty turns, interrupted by a leveling off and by mature sastrugi, the anvil-like snow structures formed by wind. Then we encountered one long drop after another until we met a run called Penny Lane, built to get skiers back to the confines of the resort. This is one of four designated runs outside the resort boundary.

Snowbasin proper is only a small part of the skiing to be found in this area. Besides Strawberry on the one side, there is John Paul and No Name on the other. With a little effort, the powder skiing here can be as good as it gets.

I'm worried about Snowbasin's future. The resort is pregnant with potential. You can feel it. Snowbasin has been sold to Earl Holding, the man who owns Sun Valley. He can feel it. It might be another case of not being content with only world class skiing. Developers need resorts with hotels, inns, shops, restaurants, and, of course, more lifts. The planned development is called Trapper's Loop, after a road planned to make it more accessible; but until the State decides when and where to build that road, things will stay the same. Whew!

The Snowbasin brochure is a sophisticated piece of promotional literature. It has nice pictures on a background of yuppie wallpaper. Don't let it fool you. It's really a treasure map to some of the most scenic, accessible, and exciting powder skiing I've found.

Opposite above left: Skiing Snowbasin's Upper Porcupine
James Kay

Opposite above right: Telemarking at Snowbasin
Frank Jensen

Opposite below left: Mount Ogden and Snowbasin Ski Area
Patrick McDowell, Courtesy of Ski Utah

Opposite below right: Spring comes to the mountains of Snowbasin
James Kay

SNOWBASIN INFORMATION

The Skiing. Owned and operated by Sun Valley Corporation, Snowbasin covers 1,800 acres with forty designated runs. The slopes serve skiers of any ability, with twenty percent for beginners, fifty percent for intermediates, and thirty percent for experts. The resort has been operating since the early 1940s, but in the last few years more and more skiers have been attracted to the large alpine area and the endless prospects for finding powder.

The Facility. Three double and two triple lifts can carry 5,200 skiers every hour along the 2,400 vertical feet of the Northern Wasatch Mountains served by the resort. Thirty certified instructors teaching the American Technique can tutor beginning skiers in the basics or advanced skiers in powder techniques. Two restaurants cater to basic needs.

Location. Seventeen miles east of Ogden, which is thirty-five miles north of Salt Lake International Airport via I-15; exit at Ogden Canyon (12th Street), then east through Ogden Canyon.

Annual Snowfall. 400 inches.

Season. Late November to mid-April.

NORDIC VALLEY INFORMATION

The Skiing. In addition to intermediate and advanced runs, Nordic Valley places a special emphasis on the new skier, offering wide, gently-sloping runs designed to see that even the first day on skis is enjoyable.

The Facility. The Viking double chair for intermediate and advanced skiers can carry 1,000 skiers each hour up 1,000 vertical feet. The Troll beginner's chair has a 350-foot vertical rise. The entire resort is open for night skiing. The Nordic Valley Lodge offers a spectacular view of the valley and a pleasant atmosphere for the entire family.

Location. Thirty-five miles north of Salt Lake City, via I-15 north to Ogden's 12th Street exit, then east fifteen miles through Ogden Canyon.

Annual Snowfall. 300 inches.

Season. December 15 to April 1.

BEAVER MOUNTAIN INFORMATION

The Skiing. While most of the maintained runs and trails are for intermediate and novice skiers, there are many acres of tree-covered slopes for the "powder seeker."

The Facility. Three chairlifts serve 1,600 vertical feet. A day lodge with a cafeteria and a ski shop are located at the base of the mountain. Twenty-eight certified instructors teach the American Technique and the Graduated Length Method. There is also instruction available for children.

Location. In northern Utah, twenty-seven miles east of Logan on Highway 89.

Annual Snowfall. 450 inches.

Season. Early December to mid-April.

Chris Noble

Pete Houdeshel

63

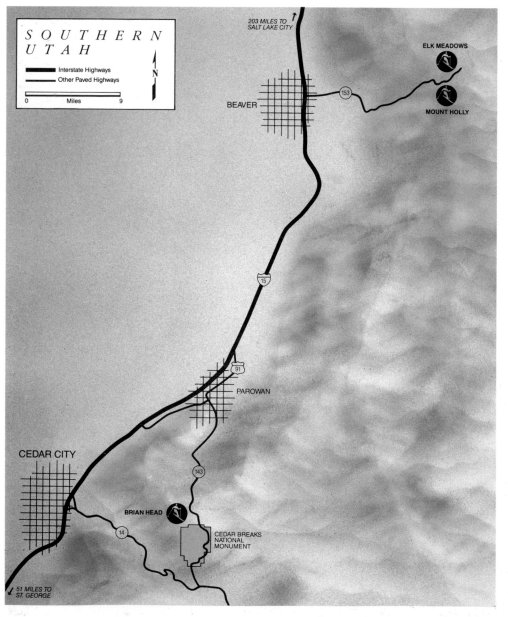

Most of the skiing in Southern Utah is done along the western edge of the Colorado Plateau in what is known as the Southern High Plateau Physiographic Region. Between thirty and five million years ago during a period of severe volcanic activity, explosive eruptions spread lava over this entire area.

This region contains the single greatest concentration of volcanic rocks in Utah, one-and-a-half miles thick in places. On a geologic map with lava labeled red, this area is a giant bull's-eye.

Cross-country skier at Bryce Canyon National Park
Chris Noble

Waxing on the Rim Trail, Bryce Canyon National Park
Chris Noble

Lunch break, Bryce Canyon National Park
Chris Noble

Cedar Breaks National Monument
Tom Bean

The Court of the Patriarchs, Zion National Park
Fred Hirschmann

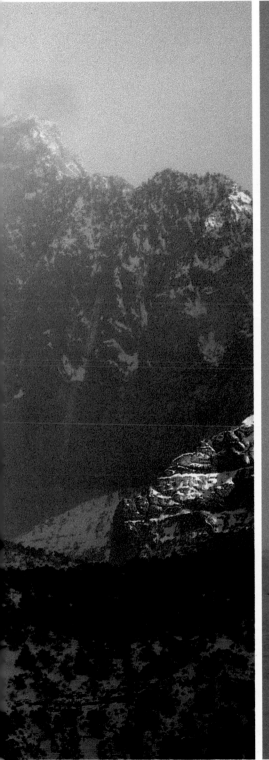

Left: Finger Canyons in
the Kolob section of Zion
National Park
Frank Jensen

Right: Cedar Breaks National
Monument
Tom Bean

BRIAN HEAD

I had traveled through southern Utah before, on my way to canyon country, but a ski resort had never been my final destination. Skiing southern Utah seemed as contradictory as climbing in Kansas, or surfing in the Sahara. As I headed into the mountains east of Parowan, I sensed the beginning of a new ski experience.

Parley P. Pratt, a Mormon pioneer, first settled this area in 1849 when Brigham Young sent him to start a mining industry. Just two years earlier, Young had gazed down into the Salt Lake Valley and declared, "This is the place." Burt Nichols must have had similar thoughts when he first decided to settle at Brian Head. In 1964, recently married and unemployed, Nichols arrived at Brian Head to set up shop. It had not been a frivolous decision; his vision had come three years earlier while working for Hughes Aircraft Company in Germany. His circuitous route to Brian Head had begun with a series of aviation maps of the southwestern United States stuck to his wall. Within an eight-hundred-mile arch of Los Angeles, Nichols marked everything he could think of that would ensure a successful ski resort. Airports, large towns, high mountains, and highways all received colored marks. Eventually, several areas were covered with clumps of colored lines and dots. One of the most colorful was Brian Head.

The resort opened in January of 1965 with one chairlift, a used T-bar, and three trailers for a base facility. Since then, Brian Head has grown steadily. Last year, on one midweek day, the resort had more skiers than it had during the first three years combined. Nichols is the first to admit that his original expectations have been met, surpassed, and forgotten. As we talked, I noticed him glancing occasionally at the area west of the lifts, a wooded hillside much like the resort must have looked twenty years ago. I knew he was seeing phantom lifts a few years away.

I was standing at the bottom of the Giant Steps Lift, catching my breath. The First Step run had been a doozy. It is one of the four or five rated most difficult at the resort. Even with the snow that had fallen in the past few days, the moguls were as big as refrigerators. More than once, my skis were forced so close to my face that I could read the mounting instructions. I had barely cleared the snow from my eyes when I was accosted by Mike Cohen, a member of Brian Head's ski patrol. "Come with us," he said knowingly. "We're going off the back." I've learned to listen when a man with a white cross on his back talks, so off we went.

We loaded onto a padded triple chair that carried us to the top, where we met four others who seemed a lot less serious than Mike. I was being kidnapped by the Brian Head Fun Team, and the allure of what I might find was strong enough to hold me hostage.

A short, low angle traverse took us to a bowl that began at the base of Brian Head Peak. Below were ten acres of that magic Utah powder I'd thought existed only up north. The last snowstorm had dropped four inches; beneath that, the wind had formed a crust as thick as stale bread. Paul, a carpenter from Parowan, was not one to fret.

He pushed off, cutting wide, graceful telemarks. I tried to follow, but the snow snakes were out, trying to trip me.

I finally fell and planted myself a body's length from the bottom, while Mike and the rest of the Fun Team hung close to the trees lining the bowl. By the time I uprooted, the team had congregated below and was admiring the tracks. Mine were particularly unique. I raised my eyes skyward and once again gave thanks for locals, those fearless individuals who have taken it upon themselves to discover the unmapped wilderness beyond boundaries and above the final lift station.

The locals at Brian Head are hard to find, since most of the skiers—eighty percent—are from southern California or Las Vegas. From the beginning, Nichols knew he had to attract and keep California and Nevada skiers. In addition to working out attractive packages for tour groups, individuals, and families, Nichols has taken into account some human characteristics to help his dreams reach fruition.

"In the ski business, we're dealing with people's egos. They will come back again and again if what they do here makes them feel good about themselves." Nichols's philosophy is evident on the resort's I-15 billboard:

BRIAN HEAD
BEGINNER TO HERO, $19.95

Beginners are practically worshipped at Brian Head. Ten years ago, while attending a conference for ski area owners, Nichols

Brian Head
Chris Dever

learned that ninety-three percent of the people who try skiing for the first time never go again. What if he were able to attract 100,000 beginning skiers and 93,000 of them never returned? He could wind up with empty chairs, vacant rooms, and an overdrawn bank account. Nichols decided to dedicate himself to the first-time skier.

The beginner area at Brian Head is separate from the rest of the resort, eliminating the embarrassment and distraction caused by close encounters with more advanced skiers. Recently completed, this area has two lifts, parking, a day lodge, shops, a cafeteria, a medical clinic, a French restaurant, and a spacious rental shop. First-timers are not only taught the snowplow, but also how to get on and off the lifts and operate their own equipment. The program is designed so that most students spend only one day in the beginner area. Not only does Brian Head make the budding skier feel good, but its lines are short and its lifts are quick. The runs are smooth to allow fast, controlled skiing. What else could you ask for?

After the morning with the Fun Team, I spent the early afternoon cruising the runs served by the Giant Steps Lift—Sunburst, Bear Paw, and Engens. Then it was on to the Roulette Lift. Straight Up runs under this lift and is selectively groomed—wide edges are left unpacked for those who want to kick up their heels in the powder. I danced down Aught and Double Aught, two tilted fairways built for cruising. They twist in and out of the trees and come together at a perfect pitch. When the lifts closed for the day, I was still eager for more, but twenty-two runs on

eleven different trails had me teetering.

Comfort was just down the road at the Brian Head Hotel, a first-class facility with all the conveniences of modern ski country hostelries. A fine blend of oak and brass gives this brand-new hotel a luxury feel without doing damage to the wallet.

I had an hour to soak and sleep and then it was time for the party up the road at the nearly-completed Brian Head Royale. The evening was quiet as I began the short walk between the two hotels; but two bus lengths from the hotel, the silence was broken by the low bass sounds of a band. By the time I reached the door, the whole building seemed to be shaking with activity. Upstairs there were a great many more people than I had seen on the mountain. There was a reason. According to one woman, residents of Cedar City and Parowan view the whole resort as a "den of iniquity;" they know that a person is up to no good when seen anywhere in the vicinity. In particular, the Royale bar is where the locals come to misbehave. I've never seen so many people having so much fun without breaking the law. Whoever said that night life in southern Utah means Family Home Evening hasn't been to the Royale.

As the night wore on, I couldn't decide whether I was having more fun on or off the mountain. But there is one thing I am certain of: When I think of southern Utah, I'll still think of canyon country, but I'll know that up on the mountain there's a first-class oasis.

The squalling ridgeline that includes Mount Holly and Mount Delano makes up the main mass of the Tushar Range in central Utah. Pronounced "Tooshar" by some and "Tusher" by others, the name comes from "tush" meaning tusk. Unlike the long pointed tooth of a narwhal or the horn of a rhino, these peaks more closely resemble molars. With broad bases and slightly flattened tops, these mountains are perfect for skiing.

Jace Romick and I began our ascent from the top of the triple chairlift at Elk Meadows. Climbing one mile and 1500 feet of moss-covered rock and hard snow brought us to the summit of Mount Holly at 11,985 feet. Below us central Utah spreads out like a wide wreath.

Jace is an employee of the Elk Meadows/ Mount Holly Ski Resort, and we are here on reconnaissance. This is the part of his job he likes best, looking for potential skiing. Formerly the number one downhill racer on

the U.S. Ski Team, Jace is sinking roots at Elk Meadows. There are few places left like this, where a retired ski racer has the opportunity to influence the development of a new ski area.

The winter has been lean and windy. Most of the snow that has fallen on this peak has been blown onto its long, eastern side. This flank, varying between twenty-five and forty-five degrees, is much steeper than any of the runs Jace and his co-workers have cut and groomed and skied at Elk Meadows. I can sense the excitement building inside him. I skirt the first pitch, not wanting to take a thousand-foot ride on my back, and I traverse to safety on a more gradual face across from where Jace stands.

Suddenly he leaps into his first turn, his edges holding securely on the perfect corn snow. From where I watch, he is a picture on a wall. For each turn, he uses a pedal-hop motion, which quickly changes his direc-

tion without increasing his speed. As the angle of the slope eases, his technique changes, and he becomes an object falling away from me in a fluid, serpentine motion. His speed is frightening.

I ease into the first of my turns on the part of the hill that is not so steep, but for me every bit as exciting. In a moment, we meet at the bottom. For Jace, after a year of hard work and responsibility, this has been his best run. For me, it has been a chance to see skiing at a level that is as high as I can imagine.

Back at the Mount Holly Lodge, it is time for Jace to go to work. Without skis, he moves with a lilting gait. Like a race horse forced to walk, he seems more at home at high speeds. Elk Meadows/Mount Holly is where Jace will smooth, straighten, cut, groom, fix, and plan. The Tushar is where he will play. Delano Peak, Lake Peak, Shelly Baldy, and City Creek Peak are good places to spend the rest of a life.

Left: Elk Meadows with Mount Holly Ski Area in the background
Stewart Aitchison

Right
Chris Noble

MOUNT HOLLY / ELK MEADOWS INFORMATION

The Skiing. For years, Mount Holly has been known for its advanced and intermediate skiing on seven steep, scenic runs. In 1985 Elk Meadows was added, with a dozen intermediate and beginner runs in natural open bowls and on tree-lined trails.

The Facility. Mount Holly has one lift that can move 2,200 skiers 1,000 vertical feet every hour. Elk Meadows has one double and one triple chair lift rising 700 vertical feet and able to carry 3,000 skiers per hour. The two resorts are connected by free shuttle service. For now, Mount Holly's condominiums and day lodge, with cafeteria and shops, serve both resorts. Skiwee and Nastar, *Ski Magazine*-sponsored programs for children and racers, are available. Watch for more here in the future, a lot more..

Location. Seventeen miles east of Beaver, Utah, on State Highway 153.

Annual Snowfall. 350 inches.

Season. Mid-November to late April.

Hiring Jace Romick is not the only thing developer Barry Church has done right. Not yet forty years old, Church's success has come quickly. The road he followed to the big office at Elk Meadows began back in the 1960s when he was one of the best surfers in the world. He hired on as an editor and photographer for *Surfing* magazine and worked winters at Snow Valley. In 1970 he wrote a column for the *San Bernadino Sun*, which sent him to Brian Head to do a story. He never left southern Utah. In 1974 Church became the first ski school director at Mount Holly Ski Resort. Now he owns it. In between, he developed a knack for real estate, marketing projects in the Lake Tahoe area as well as in Utah. Church has found the perfect life-style for himself: ski and sell.

Barry and his company, Leisure Sports, Inc., also own the six hundred acres that make up Elk Meadows. Designers from J.J. Johnson and Associates, of Deer Valley fame, have created a beginner and intermediate resort at Elk Meadows, the perfect complement to the more advanced skiing at Mount Holly, a mile down the road. Future plans include more lifts for more advanced skiing in the open bowls above Elk Meadows, a golf course, a health club, and a slough of condos.

Powder tomorrow? I am skeptical. The last three weeks of spring-like weather have doused all hope for powder skiing. At 8:00 p.m. I step outside. Clouds and wind race across the landscape, as unexpected and violent as smoke from a forest fire. In ten minutes, snow grains rattle at my window. Outside, blowing snow is making forms of the wind—a flock of giant birds or hoodoos mounting a charge. I fall asleep wondering if the storm will last.

The next morning, six inches of snow cover the wooden deck outside my window. I hurry into my clothes and rush outside to ski, not realizing that it is barely light and the lifts will not be running for two hours. I can't wait. I strap on my skis and take three shots down the short run from the lodge to the bottom of the Mount Holly Lift. The snow is perfect and just deep enough to obscure the hard results of the warm weather.

Three hours later, I am skiing silently through the new snow toward Lake Peak which overlooks Elk Meadows. From the top of the triple chair, I climb for thirty minutes to a place on Lake Peak's shoulder where a future lift will be. Stopping to catch my breath, I notice that the view is obscured by the same storm that has continued to pile up the soft snow I will ski in. For me, the Tushar Range is new and unexpected. In this modern world, a surprise like this is an elixir. I take off floating down the hillside just to confirm it.

II. SKIING THE BACKCOUNTRY

GUIDED BACKCOUNTRY SKIING
ON YOUR OWN IN THE BACKCOUNTRY

Upper Maybird Gulch and Pfeiferhorn west of Snowbird
Chris Noble

SKIING THE BACKCOUNTRY

The Ski Utah drawing that appears in much of Utah's promotional ski literature and on page 16 of this book shows the entire spine of the state of Utah from a point about ten miles above the Idaho state line to the Utah-Arizona border. The purpose is to show Utah's ski resorts in relation to each other and to major cities and other reference points. By a great degree, most of the snow-covered mountains and valleys have no printing on them. Some maps or depictions of Utah's geography and landscape will have you believe that the blank spots are not worth much. But these blank spaces are Utah backcountry. To me, they represent unlimited freedom and possibility.

As I see it, the question is not whether to ski the backcountry or to ski the resorts. It is more the difference between skiing powder or packed snow. In the backcountry, the powder is all but guaranteed. And while it varies in quality, powder snow at its worst is more exciting to ski than packed snow, which is like eating spam.

And moguls. I hate moguls. I admit I don't ski bumps well. It may be I am jealous and afraid to admit that I would love to ride across their tops like those free-style machines; with Gabriel shocks for thighs, waving arms like a coot trying to fly. I doubt it. The snow is natural, but the bumps have been carved by the relentless scraping of thousands of steel edges. The sound skis make on moguls is like a dull knife being pulled across a large bone. The snow is used. Like an old tea bag, it has lost its flavor.

In the backcountry, I can find as many different conditions as I am willing to look for—from a sun-hardened shell to wind-furrowed pockets of sugar, as hard as a rock or as soft as a cloud. It could be wet or dry. Some days, every turn is a fight; I win some and lose some. Other times, in soft, dry and perfect snow, I turn like the wind moving across a field of high grass. Whatever the conditions, at day's end a new spirit has entered me.

Superior Ridge and the Pfeiferhorn in background, Little Cottonwood Canyon
Rick Reese

Breaking trail beneath the Pfeiferhorn
Chris Noble

Summit of Mount Superior on divide between Big and Little Cottonwood Canyons
Chris Noble

78

Two photos at left: Wasatch Citizens' Series nordic race, White Pine Touring Center. Park City, Utah

Chris Noble

Three photos at right: Power skating

Chris Noble

TRACK RACING

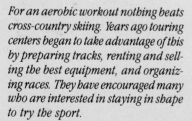

For an aerobic workout nothing beats cross-country skiing. Years ago touring centers began to take advantage of this by preparing tracks, renting and selling the best equipment, and organizing races. They have encouraged many who are interested in staying in shape to try the sport.

Over a dozen races are now scheduled each winter in the Wasatch Citizens' Series. The more than one hundred people who enter the fifteen different racing classes illustrate that cross-country racing is no longer just a way to keep fit during the winter.

Every weekend on one of four different superbly prepared tracks, skiers of every ability can be seen testing their conditioning and technique: leather-lunged endorphin junkies, novices whistling the sweet strains of the citizens' shuffle, or Scandinavians who fly like swift birds. The races are set up on a point system, with awards given to those with the most points in each class. There is also a year-round "mountain series" which encourages runners to compete at skiing and skiers to compete at running, with points given in both sports.

This is serious business. The fitness phenomenon and the sport's competitive nature combine to create a lifestyle for many cross-country racers. They can be seen racing around the courses, perfecting their technique, and enhancing their conditioning. Part of the allure is that one doesn't need to be a gifted athlete to participate. The techniques involved are merely extensions of natural movement. For many who have hesitated to try other types of skiing, cross-country ski racing has become a good reason to welcome winter.

GUIDED BACKCOUNTRY SKIING:

I. WOLF CREEK TOURS

You can ski the Utah backcountry with a professional guide or you can ski it on your own. If you use a guide, you have a further choice between a mechanized or an unmechanized trip. Wolf Creek Tours is mechanized; Guideworks is not.

Getting people into the backcountry is becoming big business. J.R. Hildebrand has known this for ten years, since he began to see uncut powder at the resorts becoming an unexpected luxury, not something he could plan on. He owned a guide service at Alta called Ski the Other Side, and friends and clients came from all over to have him lead them into his secret stashes of powder. It worked for a while. "The resorts have the attitude that if they show the people everything, they'll just get into trouble," he told me. J.R. knew that the map of Alta showed only forty percent of the mountain. His clients paid him to know the rest.

Before long, throngs of people knew J.R.'s secrets. He could no longer depend on Alta to supply the powder he needed to keep his business going. So he closed up and began planning his next venture. He had learned a lot about people and skiing, and he knew that no price was too high for a unique experience. People didn't like to sweat, and they would stand in line waiting for a guide to show them Utah powder. He also knew that there were now only two ways to get to powder: you walk or you fly. But people who paid didn't want to walk and helicopter

Opposite above left
Dennis Turville

Opposite above right: Wolf Creek Adventures' Swedish Hagglands
Chris Noble

Opposite below left
Chris Noble

Opposite below right
Rick Reese

Above: Inside the Swedish Hagglands
Chris Noble

Below: Telemarking backcountry powder
Chris Noble

skiing was too expensive and unpredictable.

In 1978 Hildebrand came up with the idea of using snowcats to transport skiers to powder skiing. After four years of planning and reconnaissance, he got the go-ahead from the Forest Service to use fifty-five square miles of "incredible, dynamite terrain." With the help of former ski clients, he bought a Hagglands, a Swedish snow machine designed to transport troops into arctic areas. He's been going strong ever since. This season marks the fourth year for Wolf Creek Ski Adventures.

From the beginning of my Wolf Creek Adventure, it was easy to see that a lot of fine-tuning had gone into Hildebrand's operation. A phone call to Park City the night before assured us the trip would go on as scheduled. Wolf Creek doesn't operate unless there is good snow. We gave the operator our lunch preference and were told where to meet. At 7:30 the following morning we loaded into a van with four men from Reno. It's twenty-seven miles from Park City to the Thackers' place, where the snowcat spends the night. I tried to imagine what the neighbors thought the first time they saw this huge, segmented, yellow bug-like creature from the next century. I couldn't.

The $130,000 machine was parked in a wide spot off the main road. I was concerned. "Have you ever had problems with vandals?" I asked J.R.

"No," he replied. "Bo and Bob guard it all night."

I didn't laugh until two dogs came over to check us out.

"Meet Bo and Bob," J.R. chuckled.

Tom, one of the guides, fired up the Mercedes diesel-powered engine, and we handed our skis up to Rick who set them in the rack on top. All prepared, we climbed in and the cat pulled out onto the road. In less than a block, the pavement turned to snow and the thirty-five minutes-to-adventure began to count down.

The time passed quickly with J.R. telling stories about skiing and fighting fires, something he and his crew do in the summer. I watched from the window as we passed some beautiful ski country. "It's better up high," J.R. informed me.

The ride was smoother than I expected. My only experience in a snowcat was in the old World War II vehicles they use in Yellowstone National Park, the ones you can't hear yourself talk in and anything drink ends up in your nose. In comparison, I thought I could cut diamonds in the Hagglands.

The road ended on top of an expansive ridge. The Duchesne Ridge curved around like a giant staircase, exposing more of Utah than I had ever seen at one time. In addition to more of the Uintas and most of the ski resorts in the central Wasatch, Mount Timpanogos hung so close that I felt like reaching out and plucking it out of the sky. As far as I could see, there was nothing but snow and sun and shadow. The guides passed out the avalanche beacons. They explained the passive control they use for avalanches. They test the slopes by ski checking, using simple observation, and

Rick Reese

avoidance instead of explosives.

J.R. has learned that you can't depend on what clients tell you about their ability, so he begins each skiing day with a test run. He took us to a fairly gentle slope and watched as we turned down it, all the time testing us to help him decide what part of the mountain to ski. We must have done well because J.R. opted for the steep trees rather than the open bowls. Not much imagination is required to see the myriad choices that exist in this wild part of Utah.

We ended our first run at a small creek, where a bit of negotiation was needed to get across. The lack of snow had left most of the creek free-flowing. Once across, the cat was there to meet us. We climbed in and started up again.

Already I could see what a big part of this experience the other people were. I felt lucky that we all had the ability to ski some of the sterner stuff. It might be frustrating to be with a group of less-skilled skiers. J.R. explained that normally there is no disparity in the groups. If there is, they divide up into smaller groups according to ability. But there's more than that. There is something about people who would spend money to be taken into a part of the country not many see. With these men from Reno, it was easy to see that adventure was a big part of their lives. Their stories rang with enthusiasm—and horror. It turns out that two of them were survivors of a helicopter crash. While skiing in California, the transmission in the helicopter froze up and they went down, leaving the pilot paralyzed and everyone else

with at least a broken back—another good reason for snowcat skiing.

On each run, we skied farther along the ridge before dropping into a new thicket of trees. Every time the cat was at the bottom to meet us. This audacious machine was undaunted. Only once did it get stuck, and then only while J.R. was trying to widen the packed road. We watched as J.R. threw his full weight on the accelerator while his paid guides shoveled. I had heard that one reason Wolf Creek runs so smoothly is that J.R. knows "when to row and when to bail."

While the runs we skied were challenging, they were shortened by the thickness of the trees. But this will not always be the case. If things go as planned, Wolf Creek will soon add another cat to its operation, making it possible to ski spectacular yet longer runs in adjacent areas—runs that may never have been skied before.

Wolf Creek Ski Adventures doesn't need to create a market for itself; it already exists. For those who have developed the tools for a new experience but are hesitant to leave the groomed but crowded resort, Wolf Creek is a baptism in the backcountry, a rite of passage. Under the tutelage of J.R. and his guides, you will find yourself immersed in the backcountry, no longer fearing the immeasurable open space, the ungrounded sound, or the wind, not caring if your legs are stout enough to stand against it. If you go to the backcounty for the first time with J.R. Hildebrand and with Wolf Creek Ski Adventures, there is a good chance you will go back again on your own.

WOLF CREEK

"Elko, Nevada, August 21, 1985—Twelve miles southwest of Elko, a fire was burning up Grindstone Mountain. As many as one hundred ten firemen were on the scene trying to control a fire that had heretofore burned 3700 acres."

What does a report of a fire in Nevada have to do with skiing in Utah? For J.R. Hildebrand, white smoke has two important meanings: it is how some refer to Utah powder snow and it is the color of smoke just before an entire forest explodes into flame. J.R. spends his winters hunting for one type of white smoke and his summers staying clear of the other. His success depends on keeping the two straight.

Hildebrand and Wolf Creek Ski Adventures have gotten off to a good start after three seasons. His "cat" is *a very sophisticated machine of Swedish design and construction; it is also very expensive. To keep his machines and equipment producing after the snow is gone, Hildebrand shoves the entire operation into a phone booth and out pops a team designed to fight fires in the most remote parts of the West. The cats are made with rubber tracks for moving people on snow and rough, dirt roads. They may be the only vehicles that can move large numbers of people and equipment into some of the remote areas where many forest fires burn.*

The people who work for Wolf Creek as guides in the winter are fit and fearless, exactly the characteristics required of a backcountry firefighter. As J.R. says, "It's a natural."

II. GUIDEWORKS

"My needs are small," I told the three guides who were about to take me on a tour of the Wasatch. "I want knee-deep, untracked powder." Dennis Turville looked at me with a bedeviled glance, wondering how to break the news to me that it hadn't snowed in these mountains for two weeks. I knew this, but I had the feeling that if there were powder to be found, Turville and his partners in Guideworks, Dean Hanniball and Ken Gronseth, would find it.

As we climbed the trail, I found that I was not paying just for the chance to ski perfect snow in a new area. I was paying for the opportunity to be with people who have spent their lives learning the mountains, the weather, and the intricacies of the snow.

Dennis Turville is so full of stories that he has to have lived more than thirty-two years. Turville never begins a story with "I heard about a guy who. . ." It's all firsthand. You will first be impressed by his confidence. Getting to know him is to realize he is as good as he presents himself to be. His talk and his confidence will surround you like steam.

In contrast to his partner, Dean Hanniball doesn't talk much; but his eyes are always moving, assessing the changing scene. I have the feeling if Turville's confidence ever started to overflow, Hanniball would be there to catch it before things got messy. He is efficient. You can keep time by his motions.

Ken Gronseth never saw a piece of equipment he couldn't improve. He made much of what he uses. He seems older, more mature; knowing Kenny is comforting. With a stitch here or a patch there, he can turn an adventure you hope to forget into one you'll want to remember.

While new to Utah, guiding skiers is an old idea. Guiding has been going on for decades in Europe, where most skiers would never consider stepping across a resort's boundaries without a qualified guide. In America, skiers are either venturing into the backcountry on their own, or they aren't interested. This makes Guideworks a gamble. Many have tried and failed to convince visitors to Utah's mountains of the unlimited, unpredictable experience that is possible in the backcountry. Hanniball believes the key to the success of a guiding business is convincing clients that the quality of the experience will be worth the physical effort. "People in America don't like to sweat," he says.

The Guideworks gamble is based on a hunch that as the resort skiing experience continues to erode due to restrictions, skiers will be looking for something new. This may take some time, but Dean, Dennis, and Ken are patient. Their plan is not to depend on the actual guiding to make their venture profitable. Their organization is set up to provide instruction to any group that wants to learn anything about getting around in the out-of-doors. They are in the process of putting together a group of people whose expertise ranges from skiing to rock and ice climbing to kayaking and trekking.

The success of Guideworks will depend on three things: a person's need for a unique experience in a natural setting; his desire to shift the responsibility for safety and planning to someone else; and his willingness to pay for it.

If my experience with Guideworks is any indication, success is not too far off. They took me to a spectacular ridge that separates Big Cottonwood Canyon from Millcreek. A short consultation determined a safe route into Alexander Basin. While they did find untracked powder, it was not without a search. Most of the snow was industrial strength—hardened by two weeks of sun and wind. Besides the long strings of telemark turns, what I remember about the tour was the freedom I had to enjoy myself. I was left with the desire to have just a small part of the knowledge these men use as they conduct their business. This is part of the plan.

"If we do our job right," says Hanniball, "people will be encouraged to learn what they need to know for their own trips into the backcountry. We would be kidding ourselves if we didn't acknowledge the dimension that is added when you are responsible for saving your own life."

Removing climbing skins in preparation for descent
Dennis Turville

Winter evening in the Wasatch
Dennis Turville

High-tech alpine touring gear
Chris Noble

ALPINE TOURING EQUIPMENT

Years ago, people who skied the backcountry did so as an extension of hiking, as a way to be in the mountains in the winter. The equipment was lightweight, not designed for making downhill turns. Today, skiers and equipment have changed to the point where people are now using the backcountry in the winter to extend their skiing experience. This is largely the result of manufacturers seeing the need for more stable cross-country equipment that gives skiers greater control. The new equipment has lured many skiers away from the resorts.

Although most of this equipment is made in Europe, it is used almost exclusively in America. Few Europeans use cross-country skis with metal edges and three-pin bindings. Backcountry or off-piste skiers in Europe have been raised using alpine touring equipment.

The skis are similar to traditional downhill skis; and the alpine touring boots are made of plastic, usually with a bent sole, or rocker, for walking. The bindings, which look like sophisticated mouse traps, are designed to allow the heel of the boot to be either anchored or free for skiing or climbing.

Americans have shunned this equipment mainly because of its weight. Lately, however, alpine touring equipment weighing only slightly more than our most stable telemarking set-up has appeared in the United States. Skis, boots, and bindings that allow the control of downhill equipment and that have lightweight and adjustable properties for climbing are perfect for those who need an alternative to the resort scene but are unwilling to sacrifice technique.

In addition to snowcat tours and guided trips, there are several other businesses which cater to Utah's backcountry skiers, including helicopter skiing, touring centers and the Interconnect Adventure.

Since 1973, Wasatch Powderbird Guides (WPG) has operated under a special use permit with the Wasatch and Uinta National Forests. Powderbirds' purpose is to make spectacular, hard-to-reach areas of Utah accessible to skiers with a wide range of abilities. WPG boasts that it is one of the most experienced helicopter ski guide services in the world. Skiers are taken up in a Bell L-3 Long Ranger Helicopter, and they are escorted down runs averaging 2,000 vertical feet. WPG guides are not only proficient in keeping clients safe but they are also expert in finding the best snow conditions. All this can make helicopter skiing an exhilarating experience. In the same day clients can ski through huge bowls, perfectly spaced trees, and gentle meadows. While the cost is high, $295 per day, you get what you pay for. Maybe more. Reservations are required, and due to varying weather conditions, a flexible priority system is used.

The Interconnect Adventure Tour offers advanced skiers an opportunity not only to ski at as many as five Wasatch ski resorts in one day but also to ski in some of the vast, untracked backcountry between them. Tours are led by experienced backcountry guides. The five-area tour begins at Park City and includes Solitude, Brighton, Alta, and Snowbird. This tour, which takes eight hours, costs $80. The Four Area Tour which begins at Snowbird and includes Alta, Brighton, and Solitude, takes six hours and costs $65. The three-area tour begins at Alta and includes Brighton and Solitude; it takes five hours and costs $45.

Touring centers offer a very important service for powder skiers, providing the instruction and guiding into the world of self-supported backcountry skiing. All the touring centers in Utah have shops staffed with seasoned professionals who can be consulted on equipment. Center instructors also teach track skiing and avalanche awareness.

The Brighton Touring Center is the brainchild of Dave Carter, a local skier who for six summers lived in New Zealand where he worked on ski patrols to earn money for his fledgling business. This center recently obtained a Forest Service permit so they can place a yurt, a comfortable overnight shelter, in the mountains between Brighton and Park City. A full day of guide service costs $50.

The White Pine Touring Center is run by Jim Miller and Steven Erickson, who started the business ten years ago by taking skiers into a cabin in the Bear River Drainage of the Uinta Mountains. They also conduct several spring tours, including one to the top of Mount Timpanogos. The rate for a guide is $35 a day.

The Brian Head Cross Country Ski Center is located east of Parowan and Cedar City in southern Utah and provides access to some of the most beautiful ski country in the state. You may have never heard of the Twisted Forest of Cedar Breaks, Lightning Point, Blowhard Mountain, and Duck Creek; but according to the people at Brian Head, if you see them in winter, you will have to ski them.

Helicopter skiing in Wasatch Range
James Kay

Interconnect guide describing route
Patrick McDowell

Brighton Touring Center
Chris Noble

ON YOUR OWN IN THE BACKCOUNTRY:

I. THE PEOPLE

A ski trip into the backcountry is a mixture of three elements: the people, the place, and the powder. Like an old family recipe, the ingredients might be reproduced but the proportions are never the same. Each trip is new.

"Never ski alone" is the cardinal rule most tourers abide by, and picking partners is an important part of any ski trip. The perfect partner is a blend of an experienced adventurer with a conditioned athlete. He can lead or follow; he will keep up, going up or coming down; and he knows new places and is willing to share them. He has dependable opinions and will speak strongly in favor of his better judgment. He can save your life. The number of partners matters only in relation to personality. Too many partners can bog a trip down, but too much of the wrong partner can ruin it.

Bob Irvine has had permanent partners for over twenty-five years. He is a member of the Alpenbock Mountain Club, which was created in the 1950s by a group of high school students. Bob and a dozen others with a penchant for mountaineering began skiing and climbing peaks in Utah and Wyoming long before it was considered fashionable. Some of the club members still live within a short drive of the Wasatch Range and can be motivated in a moment to climb, ski, run a river, or just sit around sipping a beer and telling stories.

One day this past winter, photographer Chris Noble and I had the chance to go skiing with four members of the old Alpenbock. We agreed to meet at the bottom of Big Cottonwood Canyon. The day was so clear, it rang. The plan was to meet at 8:00 a.m., but according to some schedule that seemed to have been set for a long time, everyone was early. Twenty-five years had made a difference in these men. Dick Wallin had become a doctor; Rick Reese, a publisher; Fred Oswald, a court administrator; and Bob Irvine, a mathematician, though he commutes to Jackson Hole each summer for his job as a National Park climbing ranger. All have families. Army surplus wool had been replaced by Gore-Tex and pile, hickory by plastic and fiberglass. What had not changed was the value they gave to their companionship. They are brothers, partners in the most profound sense.

We drove to the trailhead and unloaded our gear. The sound of locking bindings seemed to signal a change of character. Four grown men, with the combined expertise to run a small city, suddenly changed into rambunctious adolescents with unlimited energy. We charged up the hill on a freshly broken trail toward Bear Trap Fork. None of us had been here before, which added to the excitement. For two hours we climbed, stopping briefly to adjust equipment, snap pictures, and take in the views. By the time we reached our destination, it was clear the Alpenbock belonged in these mountains. Together, they grew up here. Their affinity with the environment was not subtle.

There was time for food and stories before the first run down—stories like I'd never heard before: first ascents, daring rescues, blinding storms, and dead bodies. "Remember when we broke off that cornice above Peruvian Gulch and rode it like a flying carpet?" Common experience had brought these men together, and the stories had bound them.

Rick felt the call of gravity first and flew down the slope in daring yet controlled telemark turns. Fred followed. Bob was just learning the turn. But his fit body and keen mind were picking it up fast. Dick laced the hill with a string of perfect parallel turns. When they reached the bottom, they climbed up and did it all over again.

After a few more runs, a couple of falls, and a lot of hearty laughter, it was time to go. On the run out of the canyon I wondered if a tour like ours would become another story. Would I recognize the story? If not, would it matter? Rick looked at me with a sparkle in his eyes. "It's the lie that lives," he said, suggesting he knew things that I was just beginning to learn.

The Alpenbock
Rick Reese

*Ski patrolman breaking cornice
to test slope stability*
John Barstow

SUE FERGUSEN

801-364-1581. Dial this number and a phone will ring inside a small cubical located among the dozens of computers and millions of charts that make up the National Weather Service. A recording will give detailed information about the day's weather in the Wasatch Mountains and provide clues about the possibility of avalanche activity. The voice you hear will be Sue Fergusen or one of four others who work with her at the Avalanche Forecast Center.

Sue talks about avalanches the same way you might talk about a book you can't put down. The mountains are her passion, and moving snow her source of mystery.

It all began with a course from Ed LaChapelle at the University of Washington Physics Department. La-Chapelle is a classic scientist involved with an inexact subject, and his students were required to sample all kinds of snow. Sue spent her field time in New Zealand, Alaska, and Switzerland, unaware that the line separating her passion and her profession was disappearing.

Sue now works three days in the mountains between Ogden and Provo and two days in the cubical. Some field days are spent digging snowpits at ski areas and discussing instrumentation and snowpack with snow safety people. Other days she works in the backcountry collecting information about special snow conditions.

In the office Sue compiles all of the information required to make two ninety-second daily messages. When information from each of the resorts in the tri-canyon area is extrapolated and merged with field observations, the backcountry conditions can be accurately estimated. Sue also does a message for snow safety personnel at the resorts, and collects slide activity information from backcountry skiers who are encouraged to call 1-800-662-4140.

During her two years at the Center, Sue has tried to show backcountry skiers how to find the calm place between acceptance and avoidance—acceptance that avalanches are always possible and knowledge about how to avoid them. With skiers venturing closer and closer to the place where high adventure turns into disaster, Sue is sometimes criticized for not instilling enough fear in those who use the system. She quickly responds that to emphasize the danger is too subjective. But to discuss the snowpack in terms of instability is to leave room for the skier's judgment and interpretation, which may lead to finding out more about a subject that we can never know enough about.

Top left to right: Charge explodes in avalanche starting zone; slope fractures and avalanche begins; avalanche in full force
John Barstow

Below left to right: Slab avalanches
James Kay, Rick Reese, John Barstow

TURNING

Every skier's goal is to turn properly. Backcountry skiers quickly learn that the ability to turn greatly increases not only chances for survival but also the pleasure of skiing. Ten years ago there were few instructors to teach skiers the proper technique, so many learned on their own. They also welcomed and encouraged changes in equipment that made turning easier and smoother.

In the early days, wooden skis with lignostone edges and soft leather shoes were designed simply to get people into the backcountry. Proficient skiers could turn on this lightweight gear, but they were ready when manufacturers came to market with plastic skis with metal edges and heavy leather boots, designed to bend only with the ball of the foot.

From then on it was a race, with the creative skiers one step ahead of equipment designers eager to find ways to make turning easy. That the designers have been successful is evident by the numbers of skiers now seen turning down Wasatch slopes. Most of these skiers are making one of two types of turns: the parallel or the telemark.

Most of the time, I use the parallel turn. I learned it first and it is similar to the turn made with rigid resort-type equipment. I love the interplay of

forces: the pressure of my lower shin against the front of my boot, forcing the ski against the snow; the reaction of the snow as it seems to press back; the action of the two forces being guided by an ever-so-slight canting of the skis; the graceful change of direction. I love the rhythm, the camouflaged force, the body's action in a predescribed sequence. It is natural, and I am powerless to change it.

Before you think my mind is closed, let me say this about the telemark turn: it is a flowing back and forth across normal; a slow vibration. Turn right for yin, left for yang. It is not without risk. The transfer of commitment from what feels natural and safe to the success of the turn is essential. It is giving up one thing for a better thing. In the midst of a perfect turn, you will be held and comforted by one of the same forces joining the earth and the sun.

There was a time when controversy surrounded discussions about which turn was better. Which turn did real skiers use? This is no longer a serious question. There is a way to turn for different conditions and moods, and most good skiers know both. What is amazing is how the challenge of developing a new skill has taken this sport to heights no one dreamed of.

There are now telemark races with sponsors and money for winners and a national championship. Skiers making both turns have skied from the tops of the highest and steepest mountains. Skiers are learning variations of these turns. My friend Murray and I were skiing at Alta. There was a foot of light, new snow over a heavy, rutted base. It was like a down comforter covering a leg-hold trap. Even the skiers with rigid equipment were having a hard time. But Murray had his own way to ski this mess. His technique is hard to explain and harder to do. He begins with a controlled leap. Then at the proper height, he does a modified scissor kick with a half twist and lands with both skis equally weighted, facing the other direction. He is on the snow for only a split second before jumping into the next turn. He doesn't do just one or two; he gracefully links ten or fifteen turns all the way to the bottom.

Learning new ways to turn cross-country skis is a form of self-expression. People learning the best way to ski the mountains are involved in a new art form. The mountain is the medium, and the artists are using their own bodies as the tools. It is a beautiful thing to watch.

II. THE PLACE

Every skier has a favorite place. Most have a repertoire, replete with tours selected for different situations. There are places to go immediately after a storm, and there are protected places to save for dry times. Some tours demand an entire day, while others can be done in a few hours. There are routes that no one would dare ski in January that are perfect for April. The decision of where to ski is usually made when one member of the group suggests a tour that he has skied before. Excited about skiing a new place, the others agree and the fun begins.

There are some days, however, when something peculiar happens and everyone in the group agrees to go somewhere none of them has been before. This usually happens to me when weather unbecoming to winter has put a shell on the snow, making it almost impossible to ski but easy to travel on. The idea of finding new areas is a

Left and right
Chris Noble

necessary part of the skiing experience in Utah. With the population center so close to so much ski country, there is potential for crowding, even beyond the boundaries of the ski resorts. Bumps in the backcountry are not unheard of.

David Baddley is an adventurous soul. There aren't many outdoor sports he can't do. There is a room in his house decorated with equipment to prove it. He is young and has yet to recognize pain and suffering—a good excuse for why he suggested we ski off Big Mountain, a place neither of us had been in the winter. There is no excuse for why I went along.

The day had an innocent beginning. We skied up the snow-covered road toward East Canyon, along the trail the Mormons came down after they first saw the Salt Lake Valley. Just on the other side of Big Mountain Pass, we entered the Little Emigration Canyon

drainage, which we would follow to the peak. We intended to ski a long, northwest exposure, ending in Mountain Dell Canyon. As we rounded the last turn and faced the peak, it was apparent that we were in the wrong place. This was Big Mountain, but the only snow clung to plants that had grabbed small amounts from the wind. With skiing out of the question, we hiked to the summit for a view.

From the top of Big Mountain you can look right along the spine of the Wasatch Range. It is a different perspective. From other places, your glance will skip across ridges, canyon to canyon, peak to peak. From here, slightly removed from the highest points, the range spreads out like a huge picnic. The length and breadth and number of peaks and canyons exhaust the imagination. There's so much skiing to do.

From where we stood, we could see some

openings that would take us into Mountain Dell Canyon and back to the car. After half an hour of breaking trail through thick forest, we arrived at the top of a long slot in the trees. Branches were hanging from my pack, my face was scratched, my new Gore-Tex jacket was torn, and sweat was flying — breaking trail, indeed.

After cleaning up a bit, we got ready for the first run. I did a short ski check, not so much because I was worried about the slope sliding (there wasn't enough snow) but to see what would happen when we tried to turn. The surface snow was soft and forgiving, but the base was tentative. I pushed off knowing that using too much weight to complete my turns would collapse the base, trapping me like a curious coyote.

We made it to the bottom without incident, but it didn't take long to find that our problems were not over. Mountain Dell Canyon, such a pastoral-sounding place, was a steep slot in the landscape, with a significant stream flowing through it. The sparse winter had left no bridges. I skied along the side for as long as I could, but the steep walls threatened to throw me in the drink. I finally took off my skis and carried them, rock to rock, down the middle of the creek. David, who had been wading the whole time, was right behind me. Aside from a few detours through thigh-deep suncrust to avoid small waterfalls, we stayed in the stream for miles. After an hour, the walls of the canyon began to rise up on both sides. The canyon began to remind me of places I'd been in southern Utah, places like Death Hollow and Mystery Canyon. Even the colors are similar.

Cheating shadows had me believing the car was around every bend. Sounds of the river tricked my ears into hearing a plane or a snowmobile. Well into our third hour of slogging in a partially frozen stream, we were spit out on to the road where it all began, bone tired.

I must have been miserable. Memories of the ride home and stumbling into the house are fogged. I came to in a hot bath. As always, the warm water began to dissolve the pieces of the trip that are difficult to swallow. In less than an hour, what had seemed like an ordeal was transformed into thoughts of a new and very different place. I caught myself thinking: "Next time, we'll start at Pinecrest instead and head for Lookout Peak . . . Maybe there will be more snow and the creek will be covered . . . Big Mountain would be great to ski . . ."

Left: Upper Dry Creek Canyon above Alpine, Utah
Rick Reese

Right: Author skiing October powder, Big Cottonwood Canyon
Chris Noble

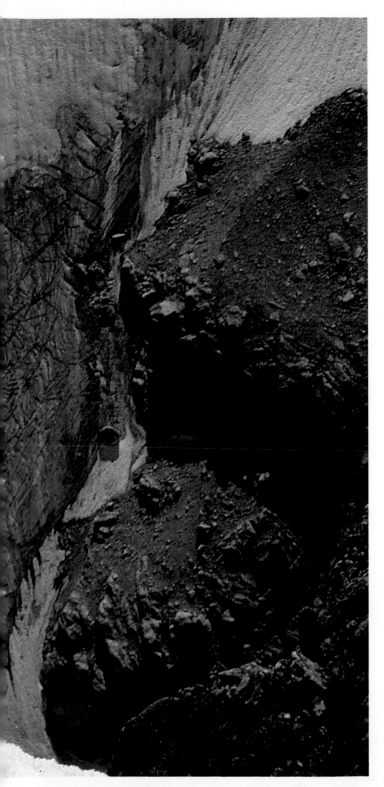

Rick Wyatt skiing the Grand
Teton
Chris Noble

RICK WYATT

Rick Wyatt
Evelyn Lees

On June 19, 1982, Rick Wyatt stood on the summit of the Grand Teton, perched against a backdrop of Yellowstone and Grand Teton National Parks. In a few moments he would become the first person to ski down this mountain on nordic-style, three-pin equipment.

Wyatt had spent four years preparing for this day. He climbed these mountains each spring and summer, studying routes and weather, avalanches and escape routes. He had honed his skiing ability on extreme routes in the Wasatch Mountains. The snow-filled couloirs of Tanner's Gulch, Mount Superior, and Timpanogos were the practice fields where he developed his technique for skiing the steep, hard snow he would encounter on the Grand Teton.

All of the training and preparation had come down to this moment to decide if conditions were right and if he felt confident. Wyatt knew from his experience in the mountains not to expect to be at his best every day. He knew there were times when one should back off. But on this day, everything felt right. He had made the decision to go and his trained instincts took over. On his first turn, he unweighted his skis, changing direction in mid-air to control his speed on the forty-five degree slope. Then he landed softly on both skis, almost stopping, ready for the next turn. His intention was not so much to ski this mountain in style as it was to simply stay on his feet. To fail at this could be fatal. Wyatt made a long string of deliberate turns down the perilous Ford Couloir, stopping once to climb down steep rock before skiing to the bottom.

Wyatt's ski mountaineering has its roots in his youth. He started skiing at the age of ten. His first ride up the Majestic Lift at Brighton exposed him to more wilderness feelings than he had ever known before. By the age of thirteen, he could be found looking for powder in the mountains of Utah. He was already developing a "mountain sense." More than a need for spectacle and risk, this sense was tied to a desire for self-reliance.

Today, Wyatt makes his living as Avalanche Control Specialist for the Utah Department of Transportation. In his office in Big Cottonwood Canyon he analyzes data from the surrounding mountains and combines it with information and weather reports that are transmitted to his computer from other parts of the state. He is an important link in the system that keeps Utah's canyons safe in the winter.

Wyatt is good at what he does, and much of his success is due to the same mountain sense he uses while climbing and skiing. Technology will never completely replace instinct in avalanche control work.

III. THE POWDER

Those who claim to ski perfect powder every time are either not being truthful or they don't ski very often. Experience has shown me what high winds and fluctuating temperatures can do to perfect powder.

What is perfect powder? Ed LaChapelle, snow physicist and powder skier, defines it as having low density, containing ten percent water. A quart bottle filled with perfect powder melts down to a swallow. Most of the snow that falls in the Wasatch Mountains is between eight and eleven percent water, but changing conditions inevitably cause the quality of the snow to deteriorate before you get a chance to ski it. "But anyone can ski perfect snow," Dennis Turville says. "The challenge is to ski well in varying snow conditions."

For me, the main element of a perfect day is finding that the quality of snow is better than I'd hoped for. One day last December, I was completely surprised.

Through November and early December the jet stream had made regular passes through our mountains, dropping ten feet of snow. But three weeks of high pressure deflected the storms, trapping fog in the valleys and leaving the mountains dry. On the last day of December, my old friends, Scott and Jim Hinckley, and I decided to climb Mount Raymond.

Left: Park City
Chris Noble

Center: Cross country skiing near Brighton
Chris Noble

Right
Chris Noble

The trail up Butler Fork is steep. Cover it with a few feet of dense snow, broil it with days of direct sunlight, and weld it with freezing temperatures at night and you've got a disaster. The entire canyon was glazed like a stale donut. In the shade the snow was rock hard as we began our ascent. Even our climbing skins wanted nothing to do with it. It was just what we expected.

After struggling for two hours, we reached the pass separating the Big Cottonwood drainage from Millcreek. We packed our skis and climbed the steps an earlier party had kicked into the long summit ridge. The poor snow conditions did nothing to diminish the experience of climbing a high peak in the Wasatch. To our left the ridge gave way to impressive chutes, pitched perfectly for spring skiing. On the right were cliffs. A fall in that direction would mean a first bounce near Baker Spring on the Millcreek side.

The feeling of arriving on a summit is always the same: elation, excitement, the sense of accomplishment as "going" becomes "getting there." It is as if I can own all that I can see: Gobbler's Knob, Mill A Basin, Twin Peaks. To the west the Salt Lake Valley is covered by a sea of vapor. I thought of ancient Lake Bonneville, with its tides lapping at the mouths of these canyons.

A quick lunch of venison jerky and Christmas leftovers and it was time to climb down. We picked a route through the rocks to the south ridge, where we donned our skis and traversed until the ridge turned to the east. We were looking down into the basin. Below lay untracked snow, three weeks old. This time of year, the sun's path is so far south that the snow on the northern side of these steep ridges is never subjected to the melt-freeze cycle. Time, warm days, and cold nights had left a layer of loose, large-grained crystals a foot deep. I pushed off, suspicious, waiting for a body slam before the first turn. It never happened. The first turn came and then the second. It was like skiing in a bowl of sugar. The base was even and firm, like an expensive mattress. After seven turns the space ran out. I looked up to the others. "It's great," I barked. They followed me down, and together we contoured around a rock outcropping. Below us was more of the same, only longer. And below that was a neat little knoll with a wide-open side, just waiting to be cut by our skis.

For an hour we traversed and skied, finally returning to Butler Fork. The run out to the car—I've almost forgotten it. I can still hear the sounds of skidding skis, the plomping of bodies hitting the hard surface, and the laughter. We had been to the top of the Wasatch and had skied good snow on a day when there shouldn't have been any.

Center: Backcountry skiing
near Park City
Chris Noble

Right
James Kay

T. G. SNOW

When the snowpack resembles sugar, it is due to the formation and loose accumulation of large snow crystals. These large crystals are also called T.G. snow, depth hoar, and pukak.

T. G. is short for temperature gradient, which is the process by which these crystals form. A large T.G. means that the temperature varies a great deal throughout the snowpack. The root of the process is in the ground temperature, which remains a fairly constant zero degrees centigrade. Early in the season, the snowpack is shallow and the air temperatures are much colder than ground temperatures. The heat from the ground begins to melt the snow crystals which initiates the flow of vapor towards the surface. This process continues until the vapor freezes into larger snow grains in the colder layers of the snowpack. The resulting snow grains are larger and steplike, with a coarse texture.

Depth hoar is the extreme case, when the grains have grown to eight millimeters in diameter. You can hold these crystals in your hand like tiny ice cubes; their irregular, angled nature does not allow them to bond well together. The pressure of deep snow on top of an unstable layer of depth hoar increases the likelihood that the entire snowpack will collapse. Most backcountry users have experienced the settling and familiar whooomph! of a collapsing snowpack on flat terrain. On a steep slope, the result is often a devastating avalanche. During some years the combination of lower than average snowfall and cold temperatures causes an extreme T.G. layer that can lead to highly unstable conditions.

In their book The Secret Language of Snow, Ted Major and Terry Tempest Williams discuss "pukak," the Eskimo word for T.G. snow. Besides being a factor in causing avalanches, it also plays a part in the ecology of a snow-covered area. The small animals who spend the winter under the snow remain very active. Shrews, voles, and mice are able to tunnel through the loose crystals in search of food. These crystals also trap large amounts of dead air, which insulates these small arctic animals.

On the surface, these large crystals can provide enjoyable skiing. Their loose nature gives in to the force of a turning ski. Other than the noise of the large crystals against the ski, the sensation is similar to skiing powder.

Skiing the Twin Peaks
Wilderness Area
Chris Noble

THERE ARE THOSE DAYS

Some days define perfection. All the elements have combined with some cosmic catalyst, forming an experience that is beyond hope and reality, never to be duplicated. A Saturday in February of 1986 was one of those days.

Friday night it snowed hard. The familiar neighborhood sounds were buffered, with the only disturbance the whirring of stuck cars. At 11:00 I looked out into the yard. The light from the house reached out only ten feet into the darkness where it stopped, blocked by a wall of twirling snow crystals. Three good skiing partners called to make plans. The forecast called for sun on Saturday, and I was drunk with anticipation.

The next day had all the signs of being unforgettable. Skiing the resorts was out of the question, since anyone within earshot of the weather report would be waiting in line to chew up every powder slope that was open. Four of us decided to ski as much of the area between Big Cottonwood and Millcreek Canyon as legs, lungs, and light would allow. We would leave at eight.

By four a.m. I was awake. The quarter moon signaled the end of the storm. By seven I was packed and finished with a bowl of Cream O'Wheat and a quart of orange juice. The sun was a giant fire in the east behind the Wasatch Range. The tree outside my window had just shed its shroud of fresh snow. It was a perfect day.

There was a line of cars in the canyon, most of them headed for Brighton or Solitude. We were on our way to ski untracked powder in a way that *Ski Utah* doesn't talk about and few travel agents understand—self-supported and responsible for our own safety, and our own experience.

Once parked, we quickly put on our climbing skins and stepped across the pile of snow left by the plow. A cold wind rippled the top, light layer of snow. It had settled just enough to make the going manageable; and with four of us trading off, breaking trail in eight inches of light snow was no problem. I was first. We moved in a line, everything we needed strapped on our backs.

My hat was the first article of clothing shed to help regulate my rising body temperature. I watched for signs that all was right with the world; the curving burrow of a porcupine between aspens, the feathered imprint of the wing ends of a redtailed hawk straddling the end of a pin-pricked trail of a field mouse. I thought about others in a similar circumstance—everyone from Hannibal crossing the Alps with 35,000 warriors and a band of elephants to the Donner Party. Somewhere we fit into this common experience. While not a life-or-death situation, our journey seemed necessary. There is something old and deep inside me that is satisfied by wild skiing, something that domestic skiing only begins to brush the dust from.

No one spoke much as we moved through a mature grove of aspens. Emptying lungs were the only sounds. We were another element added to the snow and shadow. In two hours we arrived at a ridge top, sweat falling from our foreheads making bullet-sized holes in the dry snow. In front of us, a huge bowl spread out. It was steep, with a foot of

Chris Noble

Opposite: Author skiing "Mill D," Big Cottonwood Canyon
Chris Noble

Ridgecrest in Central Wasatch
Chris Noble

new, untouched snow, and crowned with a six-foot cornice. We rested and drank in the view. A lone coyote had been there before us.

"There is no such thing as the west anymore—It's a dead issue." This line from Sam Shepherd's play, *True West*, refers to wilderness. It is a view shared by many. The wilderness is gone and with it the adventurers who took it upon themselves to discover it. But in front of us were two acres of white, untouched wilderness. Our tracks

would only be a temporary intrusion.

Skins off and Gore-Tex shells on, we were ready for the first run. In these moments, the excitement is peppered with a familar sense of danger. As with a worn wallet, shaped like my backside, I am uncomfortable when this sense is missing. This bowl had avalanched before, but on this day it seemed safe. Just in case, we went through the ritual—check Pieps (the electronic devices worn to help locate a skier buried by a slide), loosen pack

straps, and sacrifice a piece of cornice. Nothing budged.

"Who's first?" I asked.

"Take it," they replied.

Respectfully, I stepped clear of the cornice and gazed around me. Ten thousand lift tickets had been bought by people who had fought for first tracks and waited in lines comparing stories. We had nothing to do with all that. We had come full circle on a journey that began years ago with people

who loved the mountains enough to brave the winter elements. There were no real choices then. People who wanted to ski had to climb. They celebrated the first lifts that ended those long climbs and they cheered each technological advance that allowed them to ski more varied terrain. For a time they were excited by the possibility of new resorts. Then there were choices. As skiing became more of a social event, it demanded more of the mountains. Many of those who loved the mountains began to see problems associated with unconstrained growth, and they slid away into the backcountry where it all began. The circle was complete.

I pushed off and took one slow turn to make peace with the mountain and to test for the right rhythm. The snow conditions required little effort from me. My body slipped into an uninterrupted rhythm that had been longing to express itself—a dance.

For me, powder skiing evolved from a luxury to a necessity long ago. When I can't ski, I become edgy and nervous. Something is missing. In subatomic physics, Fritof Capra wrote in *The Turning Point*, "The interrelations and interactions between the parts of the whole are more fundamental than the parts themselves. There are no dancers, there is only the dance." I think it is the same with powder skiing.

One of those days
Brooke Williams

III. CONCLUSION

CONCLUSION

It is spring. Alta has closed for the season, but not for lack of snow. I am climbing the mountains which only weeks before teemed with tanning skiers. There are good reasons to ski in the spring, when nature takes back the mountain from the activity that has borrowed it for the winter. Warm days and cold nights have turned the snowpack into a dense, thick mat with no signs that skiers have ever been here. The snow gives way to boulders and limbs spring free from the weight that has held them for half a year. Ground squirrels break through the snow for the first time since fall when they began their hibernation.

One of the best reasons for spring skiing is corn snow, a magical surface that forms when the sun penetrates the surface that was stiffened the night before. Like powder, perfect corn snow eliminates itself as an excuse in skiing. The responsibility is transferred to technique and terrain, and the snow becomes the medium in which an experience can develop. As I climb, the sun heats the air and drops of sweat form on the end of my nose. The trees stand in their own shadows. The only sound is of climbing skins sliding across the large snow crystals, like a stiff brush on an old coat.

I set out in the fall to define the Utah Ski Experience, but I am confused by the web of dimensions that comprise the attraction of skiing. To make some sense of what I have seen, I look at the faces, places, events, and feelings in terms of a natural progression.

To many, "progress" must be joined with other words before it has significance. When combined with "blind" or "inspired," the word can conjure two completely different feelings. So it is with the progress of skiing in Utah.

Dick Bass knows about progress. This fifty-six-year-old businessman with a touch of Texas crude in his blood has been the catalyst and the main element in the rise of Snowbird Ski Area. "Old Large Mouth," as his close friends call him (referring to his undaunting enthusiasm for whatever interests him), has been involved with Snowbird since 1969 when he met Ted Johnson and the dream formed. Today, Bass is in debt for over thirty million dollars for Snowbird's progress.

In 1979 Bass took his four children on a five-month odyssey of climbing, swimming, and running, following in the footsteps of his favorite adventurer, Richard Haliburton. He came home knowing about the value of adventure and with a tangible sense of accomplishment. Since then, Bass has climbed the highest mountain on each of the seven continents, an experience that has reinforced and crystallized things he has always known: attitude is more important than what happens; failure is omission; and if you never stop, you don't get stuck.

Rick Reese

I asked Dick Bass about his dreams for the Wasatch. "The biggest mountain in my life," he said, "is finishing Snowbird."

His long-range plans are to create a center for human understanding at Snowbird, a Renaissance Center that will include skiing, the performing arts, and mountaineering. But it is Bass's short-range plans for Snowbird which have many people watching. "I would be letting the skiing world down if I don't try and develop White Pine Canyon," Bass told me. "Expanding the ski area is the only way to provide the financial foundation for the Renaissance Center. If I didn't have this philosophy and dream, I wouldn't have stayed in Snowbird this long."

There is a poster showing a gorilla with a dollar sign on its chest carrying skis through the mountains. The caption reads,

HELP! SAVE OUR CANYONS

"Save Our Canyons" is a group formed of people who believe that further progress in the development of Utah's canyons for skiing is wrong. Alexis Kelner has been the outspoken conscience of this group since it was formed in oppositon to Utah being considered for the 1976 Olympics. It was thought that the development required to hold the Olympics would be detrimental to the pristine quality of the canyons. Recently the group opposed a new sewer in Big Cottonwood Canyon, the bid for the 1992

Patrick McDowell

Olympics, and Snowbird's expansion into White Pine, the wild canyon west of the resort, adjacent to the Lone Peak Wilderness Area. Kelner's political activism has its deep roots in the ski mountaineering and wandering he has done in the Wasatch Mountains since he came to America and Utah in 1950 when World War II forced his family from their home in Latvia. After attending the University of Utah, where he studied chemistry and journalism, Alexis became a freelance scientific illustrator and writer. In 1975 he coauthored *Wasatch Tours*, and in 1980 he wrote *Skiing in Utah—a History*.

His wide-eyed wittiness and emotional tirades illustrate the knack he has for knowing what works in the political meanderings of Utah.

I asked Alexis about his dream for the Wasatch Mountains. "I would like to see fences put up around all the resorts so that no one could get out to mess up the rest of the mountains." He grinned and laughed. I knew there was more.

By the time we had finished talking, Alexis had conveyed to me that deep in his big heart, he believes that wild nature cannot be improved upon. Development defiles nature. He believes that the recreational needs of people can be met without cement and steel.

Even when parallel lines are extended indefinitely, they never meet. It may appear

that Bass and Kelner could never agree about how the Wasatch Mountains should be treated. But some would argue that Kelner and Bass are not traveling on parallel lines. Looking far enough into each of their most pure intentions, we might find some similarities. We might discover that what Kelner knows about the value of unencumbered wild spaces is what Bass is hoping to expose the world to with his center for understanding. These two men may be pursuing different ways of achieving the same thing. It is up to those who live near and move about in these mountains to decide which path should be followed.

I have made some progress toward some understanding of my own. I began this book with a preconceived bias toward backcountry skiing. But I've come to believe that resort skiing can be a natural predecessor to backcountry skiing. As skiers discover the joy of moving freely in the powder that has accumulated overnight on groomed runs, they begin testing themselves off the trails. First they keep to the trees and then move cautiously to the steeper, open bowls. Finally, they advance to the backcountry and an inexhaustible source of powder.

This perspective gives resort skiing new significance. Just as a swimming pool provides a safe environment allowing swimmers to gain confidence before entering the sea, ski resorts are training grounds for skiers

to learn technique and get a feel for what mountains can do for the soul. Resorts are also the place to learn about risk. Anyone who has ever stepped onto a pair of skis knows that skiing is full of personal risk. But it is a risk rooted in personal rewards—rewards that are difficult to categorize and that are different for each person. The life containing risk is more interesting than the one that doesn't. Risk is part of the allure of skiing.

My attitudes about powder skiing haven't changed. Within resort boundaries, luck is the main element in finding powder, and luck is running out. If, as Dolores LaChapelle contends, there are lessons to be learned from skiing powder, then powder is a resource that must be treated with respect. The same argument can be made for preserving powder as for preserving open space and natural areas. Powder snow is a resource that is found in abundance only in the backcountry. Limiting the expansion of ski resorts and saving the backcountry is preserving what is rare. It is a gesture of hope full of acumen, a gift to our children—and theirs. The spiritual values to be found in the mountains and canyons of the Wasatch transcend anything that larger resorts can provide.

Used snow
Chris Noble

Urban lift lines
Patrick McDowell

Years of skiing Utah's resorts have shown me what superb facilities we have to complement our spectacular terrain. Utah's mountains have something to offer every type of skier on any budget—and generally without being smothered with too many people. I think that further enlargement of resort boundaries is needless. Enough is enough. If resorts need expanding, we can do it with our own legs.

Standing on Alta's Point Supreme, the sun filters through hovering clouds, cloaking trees and rocks in a sensuous aura. The touch of unaltered breezes bites at bare skin. Mountains are the symbolic contact between heaven and earth. For a few borrowed moments, I am part of that connection. If I am respectful, I will leave nothing with this mountain. What I take will feed a place inside of me. This mountain and all mountains are important in themselves. They have a right to remain unaltered.

The chill in my body reaches a standoff and it is time to go. With one skating step I am on my way across the fast surface.

Is it the action of skiing that injects me with the passion I have for the sport? I don't think so. Action begins and ends with a precise movement. But it is momentum that moves on like a river, carrying us from season to season, building a plateau of one event atop another. Action makes us forget for a moment. Momentum heals, then inspires. Skiing is action. Skiing in Utah is momentum.

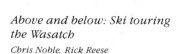

Above and below: Ski touring the Wasatch
Chris Noble, Rick Reese

Opposite above left: Mountain goats in the Wasatch Range
John Barstow

Opposite above right: Snowbird Tram
Chris Noble

Opposite below left: Lone Peak Wilderness Area
John Barstow

Opposite below right: Snowbird
Chris Noble

THE AUTHOR

Brooke Williams is a native of Utah who has skied Utah's backcountry for years with a passion for powder. His articles have appeared in *Outside* and *Ski* magazines, as well as *The Wasatch Sports Guide* where he is an associate editor. He lives in Salt Lake City with his wife, Terry Tempest Williams.

Brooke Williams
Chris Noble

THE PHOTOGRAPHER

Chris Noble is a writer and photographer specializing in outdoor and wilderness subjects. He is a contributing photographer with *Powder* magazine. His work has appeared in *Outside, Backpacker, La Neige* (France), and *Geo* magazines, both editorially and in advertising. He is the founding editor of Utah's *Wasatch Sports Guide*. He lives in Salt Lake City with his wife and daughter.

Chris Noble
Terry Newfarmer

Left and center
Fred Hirschmann

Right
Chris Noble

Patrick McDowell

ACKNOWLEDGMENTS

I wish to acknowledge the people who have been my mentors: the staff of the Utah Geographic Series who have spent enough time studying the geography of Utah to know what this series needs to say, and whose fastidious attention to the details of the business of publishing have let them say it; Chris Noble and the other photographers who have sacrificed many runs down perfect powder slopes, waiting with frozen fingers for the photographs that so beautifully enhance this book; Sue Fergusen, Alf Engen, Earl Miller, Dolores LaChapelle, Alexis Kelner, Dick Bass, Junior Bounous, Onno Weiringa, Bill Hamilton, Rick Wyatt, J.R. Hildebrand, Jace Romick, Barry Church, and all the other ski people who not only helped me understand what the Utah ski experience really is but also showed me what amazing things can happen to people who spend their lives skiing; Rosemary and Rex Williams, parents who with their love, hope, and encouragement have broken the perfect trail for me; and Terry Tempest Williams, who knew what this book was about long before I did.

Portions of this book were originally written for *Ski Magazine* and *The Wasatch Sports Guide* where they appeared in different form.

Following Page
Alexis Kelner

A P P E N D I X

Alta Ski Lifts
Alta, Utah 84092
(801) 742-3333

Beaver Mountain Ski Area
1045 ½ North Main 4
Logan, Utah 84321
(801) 753-0921

Brian Head Ski Area
P.O. Box 8
Brian Head, Utah 84719
(801) 677-2035

Brighton Ski Bowl
Brighton, Utah 84121
(801) 359-3283

Brighton Touring Center
P.O. Box 17848
Brighton, Utah 84117
(801) 531-9171

Deer Valley Ski Area
P.O. Box 1525
Park City, Utah 84060
(801) 649-1000

Elk Meadows
P.O. Box 511
Beaver, Utah 84713
(801) 438-5030

Guideworks
Box 8635
Salt Lake City, Utah 84108
(801) 363-5640

Mt. Holly Ski Area
P.O. Box 511
Beaver, Utah 84713
(801) 438-5030

Nordic Valley Ski Area
P.O. Box 178
Eden, Utah 84310
(801) 745-3511

Park City Ski Corp.
P.O. Box 39
Park City, Utah 84060
(801) 649-8111

ParkWest Ski Area
P.O. Box 1598
Park City, Utah 84060
(801) 649-8305

Powder Mountain Ski Area
P.O. Box 68
Eden, Utah 84310
(801) 745-3771

Ski Utah
307 West 200 South, Suite 5005
Salt Lake City, Utah 84101
(801) 533-4434

Snowbasin Ski Area
P.O. Box 348
Huntsville, Utah 84317
(801) 399-1136

Snowbird Corp.
Snowbird, Utah 84092
(801) 742-2000

Solitude Ski Area
P.O. Box 17557
Salt Lake City, Utah 84117
(801) 534-1400

Sundance Ski Area
P.O. Box 837
Provo, Utah 84601
(801) 225-4100

Wolf Creek Ski Adventures
5489 Cyclamen Cove
West Jordan, Utah 84084
(801) 649-2200

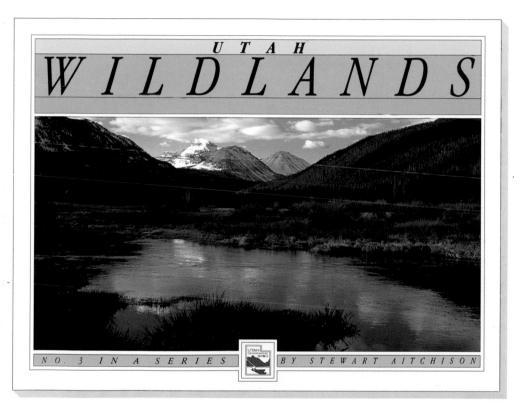

Stewart Aitchison, author of *A Naturalist's Guide to Hiking the Grand Canyon* and *A Naturalist's San Juan River Guide,* turns his attention to the wilderness areas of Utah and to the millions of acres currently being considered for wilderness. 150 color photographs and beautiful maps make *Utah Wildlands* a valuable reference for everyone who shares an interest in Utah's vast wildland treasure.

Ted Wilson, former Mayor of Salt Lake City, writes of life along Utah's Wasatch Front, one of America's fastest-growing metropolitan areas. Explore the remarkable contrast of city and wilderness, basin and range, and problems and promise through the authoritative text, maps, charts, and nearly 150 color photographs of *Utah's Wasatch Front.*

NOW AVAILABLE...
UTAH CANYON COUNTRY

THE FIRST VOLUME IN THE UTAH GEOGRAPHIC SERIES

"...the best overview since Gregory Crampton's Standing Up Country*"*
On Public Lands

"You can almost walk right into the desert studying [these photos]. You find yourself wondering why you're not there."
Joe Bauman
Deseret News

"As a guidebook and a pictorial essay, it is stunning and masterfully done...It is a must for your library."
Rose Gilchrist
Wasatch Sports Guide

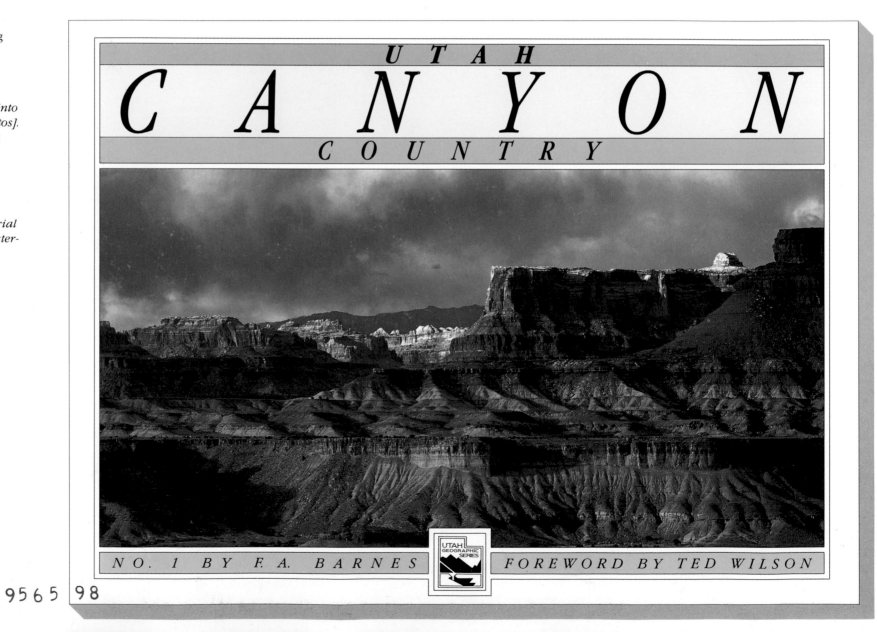

28

NOW AVAILABLE FROM THE UTAH GEOGRAPHIC SERIES, BOX 8325, SALT LAKE CITY, UTAH 84108